THE ABOLITION OF THE STATE

Anarchist & Marxist Perspectives

Wayne Price

authorHOUSE®

AuthorHouse™
1663 Liberty Drive, Suite 200
Bloomington, IN 47403
www.authorhouse.com
Phone: 1-800-839-8640

AuthorHouse™ UK Ltd.
500 Avebury Boulevard
Central Milton Keynes, MK9 2BE
www.authorhouse.co.uk
Phone: 08001974150

First published by AuthorHouse 10/16/2007

ISBN: 978-1-4343-1696-7 (sc)

Printed in the United States of America
Bloomington, Indiana

This book is printed on acid-free paper.

CONTENTS

PART I: Instead of the State

CHAPTER 1. PUTTING THE STATE INTO THE MUSEUM OF ANTIQUITIES

Anarchists advocate the abolition of the state--the basic structures of government--and its replacement by a stateless society. Marxists advocate the abolition of the existing, capitalist, state, and its replacement by a temporary workers' state which would "wither away" into a stateless society. Both would agree with the statement of Marx's co-thinker, Frederick Engels, in *The Origins of the Family, Private Property, and the State*, "The society which organizes production anew on the basis of free and equal association of the producers will put the whole state machinery where it will then belong--into the museum of antiquities, next to the spinning wheel and the bronze ax" (1972; p. 232).

Anarchists and Marxists are not only against the state. They agree that, as Engels' statement implies, the end of the state must be associated with the dismantling of the capitalist economy, the end of exploitation of the working class, and the abolition of class society. They are for its replacement by a collectivized economy with cooperative labor. This is the "free and equal association of the producers," otherwise called *socialism* or *communism*. While the term "socialism" is often used today to mean state ownership (more accurately, the program of "state socialism"), the mainstream of anarchism has always presented itself as the left wing of the socialist movement.

This also means identifying the modern working class as central to the overthrowing of capitalism. It is through the capital/ labor process that the products and services necessary for society to survive are produced, which makes the workers central to the functioning of capitalism. It means that the workers are strategically placed to stop this society and to start up a new one. The workers are exploited by the capitalists, which gives the workers the major interest in ending exploitation--and in ending classes altogether (if they see fit). Not all anarchists and Marxists agree about this, but it has been the view of anarchist-communists and anarchist-syndicalists as well as of Marx and Engels--if not of such Marxists as Herbert Marcuse or Mao Tse-Tung.

Besides being against the state and capitalism, anarchists have opposed all forms of domination and oppression: the rule of men over women, of European-Americans over African-Americans, of Anglos over Latinos, of the imperialist nations over oppressed nations, of straights over Gay men, Lesbians, and Transgendered people, of the mainstream over political or religious minorities, and so on. The record of Marxists is more mixed, but generally they have opposed many, if not all, forms of oppression. While agreeing that the working class is central to the overturn of *capitalism*, most anarchists and Marxists today believe that these other forms of oppression are also real--overlapping and interacting with capitalist exploitation. The fights against these nonclass forms of oppression are essential aspects of the struggle for a "free and equal association."

(By modern workers--or "proletariat"--I mean those who sell their ability to labor for money offered by the owners of the means of production, the capitalists. Those who work for wages or salaries, who produce the goods and services--commodities--of society, and who do not have employees under them, are the workers, the "proletarians." This was the name for the lower class in ancient Rome; it meant "those who [do nothing but] reproduce." Bitterly, the term was picked by Marx to designate the modern working class of capitalism. If we also include those who are dependent on the employed workers, such as homemakers and children, and also include retirees and the unemployed, then we have the whole working *class*. Similarly, "bourgeoisie" and "capitalist class" are interchangeable terms, as are "bourgeois" and "capitalist," referring to the "community" of rich corporate businesspeople. There is also a middle layer of managers, who run things for the capitalists. Their lower ranks merge into the higher ranks of the working class, such as white-collar workers. These middle social layers are sometimes called the "middle class," although they are not really an independent class.)

* * *

However, while anarchists and Marxists have opposed capitalism and other forms of oppression, the issue of the state is a defining question. Where a political grouping stands on the question of the state determines much about who it is. As one Marxist theorist wrote, "...It is Marx's theory of the state which distinguishes the true Marxist from the false" (Hook, 2002, p. 270), and similar comments have been made about anarchists.

There are those who accept the existing state and seek only to make it more democratic and use it to tame the excesses of capitalism (filing down the rough edges of the chains). These are the liberals. There are those who believe that the existing state may be used to gradually change capitalism into socialism, by means of nationalizing the corporations or by other forms of intervention into the economy. These are the reform socialists or social democrats (who may call themselves "democratic socialists"). The liberals and social democrats overlap.

Then there are those called revolutionary socialists or communists. They aim to overthrow the existing state. They may support struggles for reforms and make demands on the existing state; what distinguishes them from reformists is that *their strategic goal is the destruction of the state*. Of these, Marxists intend to replace the existing state with a new state--the "workers' state" or "dictatorship of the proletariat" (although I shall show that these concepts were more ambiguous than they may seem--for Marx and Engels, if not for later Marxists). Various nationalists of oppressed nations or races have a similar goal of creating new states (often they have been influenced by varieties of state socialism). Anarchists, on the contrary, plan to go immediately into a stateless society.

Put another way, socialists may be divided between those who wish to create a new society by using the state--either the existing one or a new one--and those who think a new society must be built in opposition to all states. That is, socialists are either state socialists or libertarian socialists (mostly anarchists). ("Libertarian socialist" is an old European term, which has nothing to do with the U.S. use of "libertarian" to mean right-wing pro-capitalism, supporting centralized, bureaucratic, corporations against the centralized, bureaucratic, state.)

* * *

Interest in the concept of the abolition of the state has grown with the revival of anarchism. When Marxism dominated the Left, the question of the abolition of the state itself had withered away. Far from dissolving, the states established by Marxists became monstrous totalitarianisms, structurely similar to fascism. Meanwhile, in Western Europe and the U.S., the Communist Parties mostly followed a de facto course of reformism, working within the existing state. Marx's and Engels' idea of an eventual stateless society became an abstract vision, a fantasy, similar to expectation of the resurrection of the dead for the mainstream Christian churches. It had no relation to most Marxists' actual programs or behavior.

From the split between Marx and Bakunin in the 1870s, the anarchists were on the far left of the larger Marxist movement. But after the Russian Revolution of 1917, the Leninists became the far left, crowding out the anarchists. The Leninists (capital-c Communists) seemed to have shown that Marxism could successfully make revolutions. Revolutionaries flocked to their organizations. The Spanish revolution of 1936 was the anarchists' last hurrah in western Europe, and it was a disastrous failure (partly due to their own errors). The anarchists became marginalized in almost every labor movement throughout the world. (The Russian and Spanish revolutions will be discussed in later chapters.)

This has changed. In 1989 the Berlin Wall was destroyed by the East German people. Since then, the Soviet Union collapsed. Its state capitalism was replaced by a pluralistic, stocks-and-bonds, traditional capitalism. In China, the Communist Party retains state power but has transformed its state capitalism into an openly market economy. Meanwhile the Communist Parties of Europe have turned themselves into plainly reformist parties, with no claim to be for a new society. What was once the other wing of European Marxism, the Social Democratic Parties, has long since abandoned its goal of a post-capitalist society--or any claim to still be Marxist.

As a result of these developments, Marxism has been widely discredited. Yet capitalism has developed no new charms. On the contrary, it has been increasingly in crisis, continuing to decline (in fact the collapse of Russian and Chinese state capitalism was part of the crisis of the world capitalist system). Mass discontent continues. To a great degree, people that once would have looked to Marxism (or to some other variety of state socialism), seek elsewhere for a guide to liberation. For example, in a wide swarth of the world, the struggle against Western imperialism has come under the leadership of reactionary Islamist authoritarians. In the past, anti-imperialism in these regions was led by radical socialist-nationalists and Marxists. (I am not suggesting that Islam is inevitably reactionary.)

The decline of Marxism has also resulted in increasing interest in the other historic wing of socialism, namely anarchism. Anarchism is no longer marginal. It has become part of the mainstream of socialism and of all movements against oppression. Along with the rise of anarchism, there has also been a growth of varieties of libertarian (or autonomist) Marxism which emphasize the libertarian-democratic, humanistic, and antistatist, side of Marxism.

The question of the abolition of the state has been revived with the growth of anarchism and of libertarian Marxism. What would it mean to end the state? How might it be done? If the state is overturned, what could replace it? Are there functions of the state which would still have to be carried out after its abolition? Is a transitional institution necessary between the bourgeois state and a stateless society? How does this goal relate to the experience of actual revolutions?

Such questions, which revolve around the abolition of the state, are the main topic of this book. Another topic is a comparison of anarchist and Marxist approaches to these questions. These topics will be considered in the light of revolutionary struggles, particularly the Paris Commune of 1871, the Russian revolution of 1917, the Spanish revolution of 1936-1939, and the fight in Germany against Naziism in the early 30s.

There are difficulties in comparing anarchism and Marxism (my second topic). Marxism is based on the work of a genius and is named after him. His books are essential reading for his followers. So are the books of other Marxists, such as Lenin, Trotsky, and Mao (for Leninists, Trotskyists, and Maoists). On the other hand, anarchism has been a movement with a much looser relationship to its founding figures and their works. No one considers themselves Proudhonists or Bakuninists. Their books are little read. It is a movement organized around some basic themes, rather than a set of propositions, as is Marxism. Anarchism is essentially a method. However Marxists are just as widely divergent, and disagree with each other just as much, as do the anarchists. As we shall see, libertarian Marxism has interpreted the notion of a "dictatorship of the proletariat" or a transitional state in a way which is close to anarchism.

I have been an anarchist-pacifist (influenced by Paul Goodman and Dwight Macdonald), a Trotskyist (a variety of Marxist), and am now a socialist-anarchist of the class struggle, pro-organizational ("Platformist"), trend. I identify with the revolutionary tradition of anarchist-communism. Through all these incarnations, I have remained a libertarian socialist and a believer in socialism-from-below. As a Marxist-informed anarchist, I believe that there is a great deal of value in Marxist theory and practice, from which anarchists should learn. Like Daniel Guerin, I could say, "I am a believer in militant revolutionary anarchism" but that I believe in "combining the best elements of Marxist and anarchist ideas" (in Avrich, 1995, p. 468). However, it is also my opinion that, in the last analysis, Marxism is flawed in several basic ways, as will be discussed.

CHAPTER 2. WHAT IS THE STATE?

The dominant power of a territory, the state is a bureaucratic-military machine standing above, and alienated from, the rest of class-divided society, serving the interests of the upper class. In *The Origins of the Family, Private Property, and the State*, Engels describes it as a "public force" which "consists not merely of armed men but also of material appendages, prisons, and coercive institutions of all kinds..." (1972; p. 230). Its officials are "organs of society standing *above* society.... representatives of a power which estranges them from society..." (same; Engels' emphasis). "...The state is an organization for the protection of the possessing class against the non-possessing class" (p. 231).

In the anarchist classic, *The State, Its Historic Role*, Peter Kropotkin writes, similarly, "The State...includes the existence of a power situated above society...the concentration *in the hands of a few of many functions in the life of societies*....A whole mechanism of legislation and of policing has to be developed in order to subject some classes to the domination of others" (1987; p. 10; Kropotkin's emphasis). (Although this chapter discusses the nature of the state, I will not review modern Marxist or anarchist theories of the state. See, e.g., van den Berg, 1988, and Harrison, 1983.)

This understanding of the state leads to a rejection of one approach to its abolition widely held by Marxists. Since the state is an instrument by which one class holds down other classes, they claim that in a classless society the state will--*by definition*--cease to exist. A society without oppressors and oppressed, exploiters and exploited, will, by definition, be stateless. While this may be a legitimate interpretation of Marxism, it ignores the description of a state as a bureaucratic and coercive institution above the rest of society. If such a repressive and socially alienated institution continues to exist, the state cannot be said to be abolished. To maintain such a state machine would only prevent the successful abolition of classes. An elite, organized around this social institution, will turn itself into a new ruling class. Even if, in theory, classes were to be once abandoned, such a repressive, elitist, institution would recreate them. While the experience of the so-called Communist states is complex, they demonstrate the truth of this generalization.

At the same time, the use of this analysis of the state simplifies conceptually the task of abolishing the state. *We do not have to abolish all need for social coercion or for social coordination. We need to abolish a socially alienated bureaucratic machine above society,* with specialized layers of officials, politicians, soldiers, and police. With the end of classes, society will no longer need to maintain oppression, but other social functions may still be necessary. As Marx noted, "...in a communist society...social functions will remain which are analogous to the present functions of the state..." (*Critique of the Gotha Program,* in 1974a, p. 355). *If such functions--currently carried out by the state-- can be done through society as a whole, then the state can be abolished* and sent to the museum of ancient history with that bronze ax.

Some anarchists have argued that it is wrong for the oppressed to try to take power. (Of course, the supporters of capitalism also agree that the oppressed should never take power!) On the contrary, I believe that it will be necessary for the oppressed to take power: that is, to overturn the old state and the capitalist ruling class and to reorganize society. But it is a mistake for the oppressed to aim to *take state power,* that is, to recreate a bureaucratic-military machine. A political system which is not necessarily a state has been called a "polity" by advocates of the "parecon" ("participatory economics") program (Shalom, 2004). Like many others, they advocate replacing the capitalist state with a political system organized through popular councils.

(Some radicals speak of being for a "government" but not a "state." But generally, the term "government" is used as a synonym for "the state." It has a number of other usages, describing its relation to the "state" as such. When I use "government," I mean the face of the state, its temporary personnel, the official administration which manages the state and speaks for it.)

* * *

For most of the existence of the human race, there were no states (Barclay 1990). Human beings were around a long time before states were created. The species Homo sapiens (so-called Smart Man) began 500 thousand years ago. Our particular subspecies, Homo sapiens sapiens, began about 50 thousand years ago. For most of this time, people lived in small hunting-and-gathering (also fishing) communities. The economy was "communist" in the sense that no one "owned" the land, plants, or animals on which everyone depended. People cooperated in gathering food and consuming it. Agriculture began only 10 thousand years ago. People lived in small, simple, village settlements, still essentially collective. States did not start until approximately 5 thousand years ago. Almost yesterday. This is important, because it shows that the state is not required by human nature. If the state has a history, then it has a beginning and can have an ending. Hopefully we can return to the direct democracy and economic collectivity of so-called primitive societies, but on a higher level with greater productivity.

Pre-state societies did not lack for order or even for coercion. All male members, at least, of the tribal or village communities were armed. Decisions were made by the direct democracy of the whole community (or, among some, of all the men). If individuals did not follow community decisions, usually the weight of public opinion was enough to change their behavior. If that did not work, then the organized, armed, community could enforce its will (often just expelling the miscreant). Conflicts between communities, if necessary, could be settled by war. This was often very limited and ritualized. In any case, those who decided on war were those who fought it. There was no specialized body of armed people standing over and above the rest of society.

States began with the rise of class-divided society. Just how economic classes arose is beyond the scope of this work (nor does anyone know for sure). Probably it grew out of existing hierarchies of male and female, old and young, the authoritative shaman and the others, conquerors and conquered, or other incipient divisions. At some point, society could produce more than was enough for the survival of the mass of people, so there was a surplus which could support a ruling class. However productivity was not yet sufficient to produce a comfortable life for everyone--that has only happened in the last few centuries, and only in potential (the Industrial Revolution began about two hundred years ago). Only a minority could live on the surplus. Society became divided into the majority who did the work and a minority who lived off of them. Existing divisions were exacerbated further.

The state developed together with class divisions, each causing the other. In a split society at war with itself, the armed force could no longer be the whole male population. The oppressed were disarmed. As slaves, helots, or serfs, the masses could not be depended on to defend their masters. The rulers developed a professional layer of armed enforcers, as well as ideological enforcers (the priesthood).

This conflict has reached its pinnacle in modern capitalist society. With competition as its ruling value, it is a daily war of each against all. The workers are in conflict with their bosses. Those with little or no money are in conflict with those who have more. Each worker is in competition with all others for jobs. Each capitalist is in competition with the other capitalists. The races and nationalities inside each country are in conflict. The sexes too; every year in the U.S. thousands of women are beaten or killed in a male war against women. The capitalists of each nation are in conflict with those of all other states; there is only minimal international cooperation (inbetween wars). Attempts at "disarmament" have always failed, and had to fail, since threatening and waging war are key functions of the national states.

* * *

It is said that the abolition of the state would result in chaos . This is topsy-turvy. It is the chaos of capitalism which requires the state. In a society of constant competition and conflict, there must be a state to hold it all together. Otherwise all will fly apart. A cooperative, socialized, society would not need a state to act as the metal hoops on an exploding barrel. It would hold together by itself. Society could use the productive potential of modern technology to provide a comfortable life for everyone, with plenty of free time for participating in social decision-making, and the opportunity for creative, unalienated, labor for all. Such a classless society would no longer need the state to keep it together.

(Incidentally, "anarchy" is typically used by the capitalists as a synonym for "chaos." But an-archy literally means "no rule." Similarly monarchy means "one-person rule," and democracy means "popular rule" [the demos = the people] .)

In a class-ridden, conflictual, and competitive society, the state is needed as a deciding, coordinating, body. In *The Communist Manifesto* (more accurately, *The Manifesto of the Communist Party*), Marx and Engels wrote, "The executive of the modern state is but a committee for managing the common affairs of the whole bourgeoisie" (in Draper, 1998, p. 111. This may also be translated as, "The modern state power is only a committee that manages the common affairs of the whole bourgeois class"; same). Only an institution above society, with coercive power, could make decisions for the good of the whole upper class (or at least for the most powerful sections of the upper class). For example, it is in the interests of each capitalist firm to pay its workers as little as possible, to maintain its profits. But such a policy by all the bourgeoisie would cause mass discontent, undermine the level of education and motivation needed for much modern industry, and destroy the internal consumer market. If the bosses of one firm realized that, they dare not act on this understanding, because it would lower their profits in relation to the profits of their competitors. However, the state can pass a minimum wage law, forcing all the capitalists to abide by it, for the good of the whole capitalist class. (Of course, sectors of the ruling class--such as sweatshop owners--will find ways to disobey the law, and the minimum wage will tend to fall further behind what is really needed. That is capitalism.)

The same is true for other actions which the capitalist class needs as a whole but which individuals and groups would not do by themselves. This is true for all manner of government regulations of industry. Individual capitalists are often politically and economically ignorant, preferring reactionary fantasies to what is needed to keep the system going. So there needs to be a state to step in and save them from themselves.

The most famous example in U.S. history was the New Deal of F.D. Roosevelt. The upper class hated him (calling him "a traitor to his class"), but he saved capitalism from its own failure during the Great Depression. By minimal state intervention in the economy, he stabilized the system and fended off revolution (although it took World War II to end the Depression). The state is not simply the "agent" of the capitalist class, but its main support and even creator. This may cause liberal and social-democratic illusions in the state. Many confuse the state's acting in the long-term interest of the overall capitalist class with its being independent of capitalism, even pro-worker or socialist.

*   *   *

Clearly I am rejecting the dominant "political science" model of "pluralism" (Dahl, 1989). This theory denies that there is a ruling class, instead claiming that there are a number of elites which compete with each other ("polyarchy"). There are conflicts within the ruling class as well as among different social interests outside the ruling class, such as unions, farmers' associations, churches, peace groups, etc., which put pressure on the government. But to claim that the strata of rich people, who run the major businesses which dominate the economy, are just one (or several) of the interests which affect the state, equal to the unions or to Gay activist groups, is ridiculous (for a thorough refutation, see Miliband, 1969). Over time, it is the interests of the capitalist class which dominate--in society and in the state (especially the biggest, strongest, sections of the capitalist class).

Similarly, I reject the traditional Marxist model of the "base" and "superstructure." This presents the class structure as an self-acting, base, while everything else is standing on top of it and dependent on it. As the Marxist historian, Ellen Meiksins Wood, writes, "The base/ superstructure metaphor has always been more trouble than it is worth" (1995, p. 49). If the state is *necessary* for the functioning of capitalism (as it is), then how is it in the superstructure and not the base? Similarly, other forms of social hierarchy than the class system are not mere superstructures: gender, race, nations, ecology, etc. These different systems and subsystems of domination overlap and interact with each other. They support the capitalist class structure and are supported by it, in a social totality. I prefer to see the class system as central to the operating of the society, rather than as *under* the rest of society.

The state is on "top" of all the hierarchical systems, maintaining them. For example, the state may have specific laws that directly oppress women, such as previous laws against abortion rights, which the Right is now attempting to revive. Even now, the U.S. state limits the right to abortion in the last two trimesters, denies the right to abortion support through Medicare, and has opposed abortion rights in other countries through the blackmail of foreign aid. But for now abortion is legal, and there are laws against discrimination against women and even affirmative action laws. The main form of state oppression of women is indirect. By treating everyone equally, when in fact men and women are unequal under patriarchy, the state reinforces real inequality. (This point has been made by Catherine MacKinnon in *Toward a Feminist Theory of the State,* 1989.) There is a famous saying, "The law in its majesty forbids rich and poor alike from sleeping under bridges." The law (the state) requires men and women alike to prove beyond a reasonable doubt that they did not give consent when they are raped. The state requires men and women alike to prove beyond a reasonable doubt, after many years, that they were molested as children. Yet women are much, much, more likely to be victims of rape or childhood molestation.

Maria Mies (1986) concludes that the capitalist process of worker exploitation cannot function without the exploitation of women by men--and that both are essential to the domination of nature by human society and the oppression of colonized countries by the central powers. There is, she feels, only one system, which she calls "capitalist-patriarchy." The state should be regarded as a capitalist-patriarchial state. She concludes, "The feminist movement is basically an anarchist movement...which wants to build up a nonhierarchical, non-centralized society where no elite lives on exploitation or dominance over others" (1986, p. 37).

In regard to the exploitation of Blacks by Whites, the state used to have specific racist laws, the segregation ("Jim Crow") laws of the southern part of the U.S. Now there are voting rights laws and anti-discrimination and affirmative actions laws. Yet the police will arrest an African-American for "driving while Black." The police have gunned down African-Americans for being in the so-called wrong place, such as on their own doorsteps or on the stairs of their buildings, bringing state terror to African-American communities. Meanwhile government support for impoverished people (African-American and European-American) has been drastically cut. So the bourgeois state may also be justly named the racist state--as well as the national imperialist state, the heterosexist state, and the anti-ecological state. When I refer to the "bourgeois" or "capitalist state," I mean all of these, the whole gestalt. I mostly use just "bourgeois state," partly because all forms of oppression are unified and intermeshed within the entirety of capitalism, and partly because listing all the correct adjectives would be too long.

* * *

The ruling class uses the state as one of its channels for spreading capitalist ideas (including sexist and racist ideas). It seeks to make its ideology the dominant, hegemonic, views of all society. It seeks to create a national consensus in which the oppressed buy into their oppression. Schools are mostly state institutions. Nonstate ideological channels include the churches, newspapers, television, movies, and sports, not to mention the family. These may not necessarily be bad in themselves, but they are all used by the ruling class to spread bourgeois ideology. If a class society is to be stable, the people must want to do what they have to do, with the state's armed forces only being used as the final resort. No society could survive if everybody had to have an armed guard standing behind them. At that point, the rulers' ideology would have failed and revolution would occur.

Totalitarian capitalist states tend to have a reigning theory, such as Fascism, Communism, or Ba'ath socialism, often claiming to be anti-capitalist. They use a single party to spread their ideology and to mobilize the masses in its support. Capitalist democracies, such as the U.S.A., also have their ideologies, if looser organized: patriotism, democracy, freedom, free enterprise, and (during the Cold War) anti-Communism. Religious values are often appealed to. The fight against terrorism has recently become important (unfortunately with help from the terrorists). Political parties serve to organize the masses behind competing factions of the ruling class. Competing ideologies, such as conservatism and liberalism, which all support capitalism, are spread. Elections are held, giving the people the illusion that they run society, that they live in freedom and have real democracy.

* * *

Beyond its basic features of armed people and prisons, the bourgeois state inevitably becomes an economic power. It must have the power to tax, in order to pay for itself, and to spend money, if only on its officials and employees. It must have the power to create legal money. These are already great economic influences. From its start, it uses these and other powers to promote the capitalist class economically. The United States, for example, began with Hamilton's program of tariffs, to protect its new industries; trade agreements, to protect its markets; and a national bank, to protect U.S. credit. These became major issues in the political struggles between the bourgeois North and the slaveholder South (which opposed a national bank or high tariffs and other pro-business proposals, such as subsidies for railroad companies). Today the U.S. ruling class is notorious for its rhetoric about unfettered free enterprise. Yet it has never seen a government subsidy or tax break it did not love. Particularly, it has benefitted from the "permanent arms economy," under which the wealth of the nation has been channeled into the pockets of major corporations: the "military-industrial complex," in President Eisenhauer's words. Under popular pressure, it has enacted mild regulations for labor rights, women's rights, or environmental protection, but gradually these have been worn down until they can be reversed. Meanwhile it intervenes massively in the economy. The Great Depression of the thirties proved that Keynes was right: it was possible for capitalism to stabilize itself at a low level of productivity and employment. Without government intervention then and since, capitalism would have long since failed. It would have been rejected by an angry working class. Only state policies of government spending, deliberate deficits, and control of the money supply, has kept the system going.

*   *   *

The state is the "dictatorship" of the ruling class, as Marx described it. That is, one class, a minority of the population, rules over the rest of the population. The state enforces this rule. The dictatorship (rule) of a whole class is not the same as dictatorship by one person or by a small group.

For example, in ancient Greece, different city-states were ruled by various types of governments: monarchies, military officers, oligarchies, and democracies. These were all ways in which the slaveholding class organized itself to rule over the slaves. Athens had an extreme, direct, form of democracy for its citizens (all the free males who were not from immigrant families; Finley, 1985). About 40 thousand men were eligible to vote in the assembly; usually thousands attended. There were very few elected positions (general was one). Most official positions were chosen by lot, the way we chose juries. This worked very well.

Yet Athens, for all that was wonderful about it, was a slaveholders' democracy. No less than the worst Greek monarchy, it was a class dictatorship over the slaves--a *democratic* dictatorship.

This is even more true for the rule of the capitalists. Capitalism has existed under monarchies, police states, fascist totalitarianisms, and various forms of limited democracy. At first the capitalist democracies would only let white males with property vote, but gradually they expanded the franchise to include all adults, regardless of wealth, sex, or race. What matters to the capitalists is their right to own property, their ability to make contracts, the free operation of the marketplace for all sorts of commodities, the accumulation of capital, and the control of the work force. So long as the state enforces these things, it is a bourgeois state, whatever the exact type of government.

Even under Stalinism (so-called Communism), the state maintained the production of commodities, an internal market, accumulation of capital, and the subordination of the working class. Although the bureaucrats could not own corporate property individually, the capital/labor relationship was enforced. This was state capitalism. Therefore it was a capitalist state, even if the capitalist class was organized differently from that in Western capitalism (a difference which was eventually eliminated in Russia).

In general, the bourgeoisie prefers a limited democracy, all other things being equal. There are competing factions of the capitalist class with alternative programs--such as those who believe that the working class should be thrown a few more crumbs and those who think they should be beaten back to their kennels (cuts in social services and increases in police repression). Through representative elections, the factions can settle their differences without (much) bloodshed. If a leader is dangerously irrational, as Hitler was, it is easier to get rid of him or her than it is under a personal dictatorship. Especially important is that bourgeois democracy gives the workers the illusion that they control the society, that they are free, self-governing, people. So every two or four years the people go to the polls and pick one of two agents of the rich to rule over them. Then they go to work and take orders from unelected bosses for the rest of the time.

For the workers it is better to live under a bourgeois democracy than under bourgeois totalitarianism. It is easier to live, as well as easier to organize against the capitalists, and easier for minority views (such as anarchism) to be heard. But the best bourgeois democracy remains a dictatorship of the capitalist class, nonetheless.

Even under bourgeois democracy, the state rises above the rest of society and the executive branch rises above the rest of the state. Anarchists expect the state to have a logic and dynamic of its own. Marx and Engels studied how the state became increasingly autonomous from its underlying classes, when the classes of society were each unable to dominate on their own--for example, when the workers and the bourgeoisie were both strong enough to present their claims but too weak for either to take over and run society themselves. Marx called this "Bonapartism," from the French dictatorship of Louis Napoleon Bonaparte (nephew of the first Napoleon). However, that the state becomes relatively autonomous does not change its essential nature as a bourgeois institution. It continues to enforce the rules of capitalism, the rights of private property, and the capital/labor relationship. It looks out for the interests of society as a whole, but that society remains capitalist society.

Reformists point to conflicts inside the state, particularly in the legislature. They note that some laws may be passed which are good for the people, such as anti-discrimination laws or increased minimum wage laws. Therefore, they conclude, the state is a neutral ground on which working people and capitalists contend. And therefore, the state must not be destroyed but made more democratic, more accessible to the people (e.g., Laclau & Mouffe,1985).

The argument is wrong. The management of a capitalist corporation may also have internal conflicts. Faced with the pressures of its workers (perhaps the threat of union organizing), management personnel may disagree about whether to give in a little or to crush them completely. Management may decide that it is better to accept an antidiscrimination clause in the union contract and to raise its wages. But this does not change the nature of corporate management. It remains a capitalist institution, the enemy of the working class. Like the state, it should be pressured from without, not joined. The record of union officials on corporate boards is no more impressive than the record of social democrats in government.

Chapter 3. Revolution or Reform?

In 1887, the British playwright George Bernard Shaw criticized antistatism, "I regard machine breaking as an exploded mistake. A machine will serve Jack as well as his master if Jack can get it out of his master's hands. The State Machine has its defects, but it serves the enemy well enough; and with a little adaptation, it will serve us quite as well as anything we are likely to put in its place" (quoted in Ostergaard, 1997, pp. 123-124). Opposed to both anarchism and Marxism, Shaw was a leader of the ultra-reformist Fabian socialist grouping. Together with the other leaders of the Fabians, Beatrice and Sidney Webb, he advocated the gradual extension of municipal and national ownership, under the leadership of enlightened bureaucrats, until complete state socialism was achieved. They laid the basis for the reform socialism of the British Labor Party (which has been abandoned in our time for pro-capitalist liberalism). They opposed the Russian revolution, so long as there was all that messy mass action, but once it had degenerated into Stalinism, they became enthusiastic supporters of the Russian state. They felt that Stalin demonstrated how well the state machine ("with a little adaptation") could serve if put in the hands of benevolent officials.

I am presenting another view. Since Bakunin, revolutionary anarchists have called for the overturning, smashing, and uprooting of the state, as part of the dismantling of capitalism. After the Paris Commune of 1971 (to be discussed later), Marx came to the same conclusion, "...The working class cannot simply lay hold of the ready-made state machinery and wield it for its own purposes" (Marx & Engels, 1971; p. 68). This sentence was so important to him that Engels and he repeated it in their 1872 preface to the *Communist Manifesto*, and Engels quoted it again in his 1888 preface. This was the *only* change that they made in this classic statement of their views. Marx declared that the revolutionary goal of an oppressed people "...will be no longer, as before, to transfer the bureaucratic-military machine from one hand to another, but to *smash* it..." (1871 letter to Kugelman, quoted in Lenin, 1970, p. 313; Marx's emphasis). That is, *once the majority of the working class is convinced of the need for socialism*, it would have to make an armed insurrection and destroy the state.

* * *

The state is a vital supporting part of the capitalist system. The rule of the capitalist class should be destroyed and be replaced by an alternate system because it is immoral. Some give orders and others obey; some rule and others are ruled; some live off the surplus and others do the hard work. This is wrong, however high or low the incomes of the workers. The basic wrong of capitalism is not poverty--although there is much wretched poverty--but domination, the rule of the few over the many. Also, it supports other forms of domination, such as the rule of men over women and of European-Americans over People of Color.

Furthermore, the capitalist economy is unstable, going through its business cycles, going up until it creates economic bubbles and then plunging downward into recessions. Since the 1970s, the overall direction of the world economy has been downhill. A general collapse into another world Great Depression has been avoided, so far, by various artificial means, including vast military expenditures, the looting of the environment, and the ballooning of public and private debt. But the danger of such a collapse remains. Meanwhile the system has been incapable of industrializing the poverty-stricken parts of the world in any solid and balanced way.

Capitalist states continue to wage wars around the globe. With the end of the Cold War, nuclear weapons are even more widely spread, while the big powers continue to hold their own nuclear bombs. The danger of worldwide, civilization-destroying, nuclear war continues and even increases.

Meanwhile capitalist industrialism continues to upset the balance of nature, wiping out species, using up nonrenewable resources, increasing pollution, and causing global warming. After World War II, capitalism gave the impression of a new era of affluence by adopting new and dangerous technologies (Commoner, 1974). In effect, the economic crisis was transformed into an ecological crisis. These effects also threaten the destruction of human civilization and life itself. Capitalism has an irrational drive to accumulate and grow (quantitatively), to make more money, regardless of the consequences to the world and to the world's people.

In brief, the capitalist system--including its state--is both immoral and dangerous to humanity. It must be destroyed if humanity is to survive and even to grow culturally. (The moral arguments made here are typically anarchist; Marx sneered at moral appeals as "utopian." The appeals from necessity are typical of Marxism; Marx said much about capitalism's economic difficulties and its wars, little about the environment.)

* * *

It would be good if a change from capitalism to stateless socialism could be achieved by peaceful, legal, and gradual means. If this were possible, everyone would prefer it--certainly I would. As Thomas Jefferson put it, justifying a revolution in *The Declaration of Independence*, "...All experience hath shown, that mankind are more disposed to suffer, while evils are sufferable, than to right themselves by abolishing the forms to which they are accustomed" (Declaration of Independence,1996, p. 4). An armed revolution is an uncertain thing and its price, in "our lives, our fortunes, and our sacred honor" (same, p. 13), is enormous. Yet the capitalist class had to come to power through a series of revolutions: the English (led by Cromwell), the U.S. of 1776, the French of 1789, and the Latin American revolutions (led by Bolivar and others), to list the main ones (I would also include the U.S. Civil War). Now the bourgeoisie has the gall to condemn revolutions as immoral! What is being proposed is an even greater change than ever before, the end of all classes and states, which will require the greatest upheavals of all.

Shaw and others advocated that the workers gradually win the majority of votes and thus take power in the bourgeois-democratic governments. Then their party can use its control of the state to introduce a socialist program, mainly by nationalizing the economy. This has been called "the parliamentary road to socialism" (since most capitalist democracies have parliaments, unlike the U.S. system). There are a number of reasons why this reformist approach has never worked and can never work.

To begin with, it is not so easy to win electoral power. A great deal of money is needed to run in elections, which gives the capitalists a major advantage. There are also many legal obstacles in the way, such as winner-takes-all local election units. The United States has one of the worst systems, with its gerrymandered voting districts so arranged that incumbents are almost always reelected; its two houses of Congress, including the Senate, in which each state gets two Senators, no matter the size of the state population; its alternating elections, so that the majority is never given a clear opportunity to make changes; its presidential electoral college, so that minorities in each state are not counted during presidential elections; its election of Senators for six years and appointment of judges for life. Besides which is the vast, unelected government: the huge bureaucracy, including both civil service personnel and the police and military.

However, so-called Socialist Parties (social democrats) have been elected in various European and other governments. Even when elected they rarely have full power (being checked by oppositions in parliament, the courts, the civil service, and the military). Even if they control the government, they do not control the economy. They have to manage a capitalist economy, which makes it difficult to carry out socialist policies, to say the least. If they are too radical, the capitalists have many ways to put pressure on them. It is dangerous for a government to "lose the confidence" of the capitalists. The capitalists can go on a "strike," stopping investment, sending money abroad, and closing down industries. The socialist administration could respond by taking over the capitalist firms, but that would be counter to their reformist commitments. Instead, whenever this has happened, they have capitulated to the capitalists, and abandoned their socialist program (which was mostly rhetoric anyway). Otherwise they are likely to be voted out in the next election, due to all the disgruntled middle class and unemployed voters created by the capitalist "strike." All this has been done, over and over again. But what if the socialists are too radical for the capitalists, or if the capitalists feel that they can no longer afford even the slightest reforms? Then the capitalists will abandon bourgeois democracy, despite its benefits for them. They may pay psychopaths to organize mass movements of demoralized middle class and better-off working class people. These fascist forces would terrorize the socialists and unionists, driving the socialists from the streets, and murdering their leaders. Racial hatreds would be whipped up. The military would be encouraged to make a coup. Elections would be canceled. A dictatorship would be installed. After the fascists and/or the military have taken over, there would be a murderous assault on the left, a bloodbath of activists as well as ordinary workers. After years of the utmost tyranny, a limited democracy may be reinstalled, now that the left has been effectively tamed. This is not speculation. Just such policies were carried out in Italy in the 1920s, in Germany in the 1930s, in Spain in the thirties, and in other European countries during that era. Such policies were carried out again in Chile in 1978, against the Allende government, in Central America and elsewhere throughout the world, again and again. The only way to prevent such fascist dictatorships is by the workers preparing to fight to defend themselves and their democratic rights, ultimately by fighting to take over and establish the self-rule of the working class.

The first election I paid attention to was the 1964 presidential race between Lyndon Johnson, the Democrat, and Barry Goldwater, the Republican. This was the beginning of the far-right takeover of the Republican Party. Although still too young to vote, I paid attention to the debate among socialists about whether to support Johnson (Harrington, 1964; McMahan, 1964). I was persuaded that the more moderate, social democratic, view was correct, that it was necessary to support Johnson because Goldwater would do terrible things such as expand the war in Vietnam. And it was argued, by Michael Harrington (1964), that there would be a "political realignment" in which the right-wingers and racists would leave the Democrats and concentrate themselves in the Republican Party, while the Democrats would become the party of the unions, of Blacks, and of progressive people. Johnson was elected in a landslide. He then greatly expanded the war in Vietnam, sending in many more U.S. troops and starting the bombing of North Vietnam. I was disillusioned-- and enlightened. It was too early to see that "political realignment" would indeed happen, by the far-right capturing the Republicans--but the Democrats, instead of becoming a party of the workers and oppressed, also moved to the right, just behind the Republicans. But I saw enough of Johnson's war-waging. I have never voted for a major party candidate since, and rarely for anyone. They cannot fool me twice.

* * *

As movements, both anarchism and Marxism have had revolutionary and reformist wings--those who aimed at the destruction of the bourgeois state and those who sought to work through, or around, the existing state. The issue is *not* whether to struggle for reforms as such, changes which would make life somewhat better under capitalism. Revolutionaries typically support struggles for reforms within the system. Reforms include higher wages, the right to form unions, less discrimination against African-Americans or women, and more civil liberties. Reforms are good for the people. The struggle for them, win or lose, may open workers up to the need for revolution. But the *strategic goal* of revolutionaries is the smashing of the bourgeois state.

There has always been a reformist wing within anarchism--from the time of Pierre-Joseph Proudhon, the person who first called himself an "anarchist," to Paul Goodman, the most well-known anarchist writer of the 'sixties (Goodman, 1994). Such approaches believe that a series of small social changes, new ways of relating to each other, new ideas, and small institutions, would gradually, if drastically, change society. Some see this as a never-ending struggle, with anarchism as a permanent opposition to authoritarian institutions (Barclay, 1990). They point out that society will never be perfect and human beings will always have conflicts, failures, and imperfections. This is true--although it is impossible to know the limits to human improvement. But it does not contradict the possibility of creating a new, vastly superior, form of society. There have been quite a lot of different social systems over the generations, from classless-stateless hunter-gather societies to slave societies, feudalism, and capitalism. Why can't there be another social system? Is change at an end? We do not wish to abolish all human imperfections; just the risk of nuclear wars waged by national states.

Other anarchists believe that the result of gradual changes will be a new society, more-or-less similar to communist anarchism. They sometimes regard themselves as revolutionaries because they wish to change from capitalism to a different society. However this is classic reformism. It assumes that there is no need for a qualitative break going from one system to another. It hopes to do an end run around the capitalist class. Assuming that the state will not intervene to support capitalism, it denies the need to confront the state.

The worst example of anarchists who adjusted to the capitalist state occurred when World War I broke out. Like the leading Marxists who supported their governments, a group of prominent anarchists, including Kropotkin, endorsed the Allied side of the imperialist war. The leading individualist anarchist, Benjamin Tucker of the U.S., also supported it. So did the French labor union federation which had been largely built by anarchist-syndicalists (although not currently led by them). Unlike the Marxists, however, a majority of anarchists opposed the war. Errico Malatesta (1984) wrote a scathing condemnation of Kropotkin and his friends, calling them "government anarchists." Altogether these events demonstrated why the sharpest opposition was necessary to the imperialist state.

* * *

The main reformist trend within anarchism has been the attempt to build alternate institutions, particularly producer and consumer cooperatives and small communes (intentional communities). Such institutions could be built for many reasons, but the reformist anarchist one is strategic: to build them so that they grow and federate until they replace capitalism and the state. This was first proposed by Proudhon. This approach does not necessarily call on the state for help (although some versions do) but expects the state to be at least neutral, permitting the alternate institutions to overtake it. Rather than confronting the state and capitalism, it hopes to peacefully bypass them, without the need for a revolution. It is consistent with those who do want to use the state machinery. Proudhon, himself, near the end of his life, ran for, and was elected to, the French legislature, where he accomplished nothing. He also was continually trying to make up to men of power, politicians and princes, to help his scheme.

Cooperatives and other alternate institutions are excellent. They can do much good for their members and for the community. There is hardly an economic enterprise which has not been successfully managed by a consumer or producer (worker-run) coop. This can be cited when arguing for the possibility of a democratic, cooperative, economy. However, revolutionaries reject the alternative institution idea *as a strategy*. (For some reason, this strategy is often confused with the revolutionary concept of "dual power," which will be discussed in the chapter on the Russian revolution.)

The main problem of cooperatives, throughout history, has been that *they fail by success*. They do well and then get absorbed into the capitalist economy, as subsidiary forms. Coop stores sell healthy foods but may end up exploiting their nonunion workers. Worker coops do so well that it costs too much for new people to join; the older members may want to sell out to a capitalist firm for a big profit. Other coops just blend in. I live in a housing cooperative. It is run by a group of retired business people and school principals; there has been no need to hire a professional manager. But, like all the other housing coops and condos, it is no threat to the capitalist system! The most successful examples of anarchist-communist intentional communities have been the kibbutz collectives of Israel. Far from threatening capitalism, they have been an important part of the Zionist colonial-settler state which has dispossessed the Palestinian Arabs.

What if cooperatives, collectives, or other alternate institutions did become a threat to capitalism? The capitalists are not so stupid that they could not realize this in time. The marketplace, even more than the state, is the capitalists' playing field. To get ahead requires fitting in. Any institution which is too "alternative" will not get bank loans, advertising space, products to buy or sell, etc. If threatened enough, the capitalists could run a propaganda campaign about the evil effects of cooperatives, which supposedly undermined free enterprise. The state could pass laws limiting them or even outlawing them. For example, a few years ago the big banks began to complain about credit unions. These are nonprofit bank cooperatives, owned by their members, and often sponsored by unions and other popular organizations. They work quite well. The big capitalist banks claimed that the credit unions were getting too many breaks in terms of taxation and regulation. They wanted the laws made stricter for the credit unions, and they got what they wanted. This is a minor example.

Cooperatives and other alternate institutions have many virtues, but as a strategy for overturning capitalism, they will not work. There is no alternative to mass, direct, confrontation with the state, sooner or later.

* * *

Anarchist reformism often overlaps with absolute pacifism. This has been advocated by many anarchists, such as Leo Tolstoy and Paul Goodman. To reject pacifism does not mean to be "for" violence. Over 99.99 percent of the human race believes that there are times when violence is, unfortunately, necessary. So do non-pacifist anarchists. Most anarchists today reject "terrorism," that is, the use of violence against politicians, the rich, police, or crowds. There was a time, in the 19th century before World War I, when a minority of anarchists did use such methods, killing a number of the crowned heads of Europe. In our time, the Unabomber, who has identified himself as an anarchist, is infamous for sending letter bombs to blow up people (mostly low level people; the rich have employees to open their mail). Such acts often drove ordinary people, in reaction, to support repression by the state (something which happened in the U.S. after 9/11). In 1891, Kropotkin summarized the 19th century experience with anarchist terrorism, "...It is not these heroic acts which make revolutions. Revolution is above all a mass movement.... Institutions rooted in centuries of history are not destroyed by a few pounds of explosives. The time for such action has passed and the time for the anarchist and communist idea to penetrate the masses has come" (quoted in Tuchman, 1994, p. 72).

Rejection of "terrorism" does not justify absolute pacifism. Nonviolent methods are often useful, even during revolutions, such as withdrawing labor in a strike, or using "propaganda" to persuade the troops on the other side. But there are limits to nonviolence. Nonviolence may work in situations in which the conflicts are limited. Thus Gandhi could force the British out of India, because they knew that they could continue to invest British capital in an independent India. But some conflicts are irreconcilable; they must be fought to the finish. Either the capitalist class will rule or the working class will overturn it and take over. There is no middle ground. Nor will nonviolence work against a ruthless enemy, such as the Nazis. Nonviolent campaigns can be crushed by an enemy which is prepared to kill and kill and kill the nonviolent demonstrators. This happened to the nonviolent South African freedom struggle in the 1950s, after which it turned to armed struggle. Similarly the Kosovars tried nonviolence resistance for years against the Serbs before turning to armed force. Had Martin Luther King's movement been confronted only by the white establishment in the US South, without the intervention of the national US ruling class, it would have been drowned in blood. Nonviolence usually uses national and international news to spread its story; a sufficiently repressive regime could suppress all news of the nonviolent struggle.

Nonviolence also depends on violence, if only in the background. The British could not repress Gandhi's movement because they were weakened by the Second World War. The Japanese army had softened them up for Gandhi. British imperialists knew that if Gandhi failed, they would have to face a violent national liberation struggle. It was better to cut a deal with the Congress Party. Similarly, King's Civil Rights Movement relied on a background threat of mass violence (symbolized by Malcolm X). This eventually burst into reality with the rebellions of the Northern ghettos (so-called riots), which won national anti-discrimination laws.. Once the civil rights laws were passed, of course, they were implemented by the government, using courts and the police, that is, by state violence. Nonviolence would have been for nothing without this violence.

* * *

Marx and Engels were revolutionaries but the roots of Marxist reformism lie deep in Marx's theory. Marx was a crusading newspaper editor in Germany, fighting for the most thoroughgoing bourgeois democracy possible against both the Prussian state and the vacillating liberals. This was true both before and after he became a revolutionary socialist (a Marxist). In England, Engels and he were close to the leaders of the Chartist movement, the workers' movement for expanding parliamentary democracy. Marx's and Engels' strategy was to fight for a radically-democratic bourgeois democratic state (which would have required revolutions against most of the European semi-feudal monarchist-bureaucratic regimes of the time). Then the workers would use their democratic rights to elect their representatives who would implement a socialist program (such as the one given at the end of the *Communist Manifesto* section II). The *Manifesto* summarizes, "...The first step in the revolution by the working class, is to raise the proletariat to the position of ruling class, *to win the battle for democracy*" (in Draper, 1998, p. 155; my emphasis). It refers to this becoming "... the state, i.e. the proletariat organized as the ruling class" (same). It was this state which would eventually wither away.

During the 1971 uprising in Paris known as the Commune, Marx observed what the workers of Paris did to reorganize their political structures--and he learned from them. Extrapolating from what they did in 72 days, he developed a deeper understanding of the state and revolution (to be discussed further in the next chapter). He concluded that it was not possible to vote-in socialism. There was no "parliamentary road to socialism." Even the most democratic of capitalist states would have to be smashed and replaced with a Commune-like structure.

Yet he did not reorganize his politics around this new insight. Instead, he increased his emphasis on working within the existing state. He proposed to the International Working Men's Association (the First International), that it seek to build workers' political parties everywhere, to run in elections. Marx and Engels argued that the Commune had shown the workers the need to take political power. To make this meaningful, the workers needed to form their own parties, separate from the various bourgeois parties, no matter how liberal. Organized into these parties, the working class would contend for power by running in elections. They got a resolution to this effect on "Political Action of the Working Class" passed by the September 1871 London Conference of the International (Marx, 1974a).

Nine years later, Marx wrote an introduction to a new French workers' party, including, "...Collective appropriation can only proceed from a revolutionary action of the class of producers--the proletariat-- organized in an independent political party;...universal suffrage...will thus be transformed from the instrument of fraud that it has been up till now into an instrument of emancipation; the French socialist workers...have decided, as the means of organization and struggle, to enter the election..." (1974a, p. 376-377). This program passed, over the objections of its anarchist members. They did not believe that elections would stop being a means of bourgeois fraud and become instruments of emancipation just because a workers' socialist party decided to use them for organizing and struggle.

Leaving aside conflicts over personalities and organizational issues, this electoralist strategy became the main political dispute between Marx and the anarchists. Marx argued that the anarchists were ignoring the importance of the workers taking power and the best way to raise the issue, namely through elections. He accused them of being "political indifferentists."

On their part, the anarchists accused the Marxists of capitulating to the capitalist state, of ignoring the corrupting influence of running in elections and, even more, of being elected to bourgeois parliaments. Elected representatives would get used to living well and rubbing shoulders with the rich. Even just running requires that the party propose policies for managing the state and for directing the capitalist economy--to start thinking like bourgeois politicians. In peaceful times, most workers are nonrevolutionary; to try to win their votes means to accommodate to their reformist consciousness. Some Marxists agreed with this anti-electoralism, such as the Britisher William Morris, who was active during Engels' later years. In building the social-democratic parties of Europe, Marx and Engels were effectually in coalition with political enemies, the reformists. That is, Marx and his supporters wanted to build parties in order to make revolutions while their allies wanted to build workers' parties in order to prevent revolutions.

* * *

It is not clear, at least to me, just what was Marx's and Engels' strategy for elections. Marx did say, on a few occasions, that he thought it possible for the workers' parties to peacefully win power in some countries, such as Britain and the U.S.A. I doubt he was right even there, but in any case he usually qualified this by predicting that this would probably be followed by a "slave-owners' rebellion."

He meant that events would be like what happened when Lincoln was democratically elected in the U.S. The slave-owners, rather than accepting the vote, rose up, taking the best military officers with them, and tried to overthrow the government and break up the country. There followed as bloody and bitter a civil war as any bottom-up revolution. In most of the industrialized world (that is, Europe, at the time), Marx believed that violent revolutions would probably be necessary, because the capitalists would not permit peaceful, democratic, changes. What is unclear to me is how he expected to get from (hopefully) winning elections to making a revolution.

Engels explained his view, writing that the workers would show their political readiness by the extent to which they organized themselves into parties independent of the possessing class. "Universal suffrage is thus the gauge of the maturity of the working class. It cannot and never will be more....On the day when the thermometer of universal suffrage shows boiling point among the workers, they as well as the capitalists will know where they stand" (1972; p. 232). Quite frankly, this seems inadequate. On the one hand, he acknowledges that voting cannot change the state and the economy ("it never will be more" than a measure of popular opinion). On the other hand...then what?

By now, we have well over a century of experience with Marxist electoralism. On the historical evidence, the anti-electoralists were right. In Germany and elsewhere, the social democrats built parties which claimed to be revolutionary and Marxist (except the British Labor Party, which never claimed to be either). They talked the talk. Meanwhile they elected a battery of politicians to parliaments, built a party bureaucracy which lived far better than did the ordinary workers, and built a similar union bureaucracy. They published newspapers and sponsored all sorts of popular clubs and societies for the workers. How any of this was going to lead to a revolutionary change was not really considered. Someday, it was assumed, the capitalist economy would have a crisis, and the workers' mood would reach a "boiling point," and there would be a revolution. Some day. Most officials regarded this as irrelevant for day-to-day action. An openly reformist (or "revisionist") trend developed, led by Eduard Bernstein, once Engel's close associate. He urged the abandonment of the final goal of socialism in favor of a limited struggle for day-to-day benefits.

Then in 1914 an imperialist war broke out in Europe and abroad. The socialist parties which had sworn brotherhood now voted for the war policies of their governments, in Germany, France, Britain, and elsewhere. This was a great shock to many leftists (such as Valdimir Ilych Lenin). Even those socialists who criticized the war, mostly refused to condemn their pro-war brothers and sisters--except for a few far-leftists.

After the war, the leading social democrats sought to sabotage the Russian revolution and then to defeat revolutions which broke out in Germany and Italy and elsewhere. The leaders of the German social democrats made an alliance with the army and murdered Rosa Luxemburg and Karl Liebknecht and many other revolutionary socialists. In the twenties and thirties, the social democrats failed to fight the rising fascists, including the Nazis (the failure of the social democrats in Germany and Spain to fight fascism will be discussed later). After World War II, they became out-and-out supporters of U.S. imperialism in the Cold War. By now they have completely abandoned any claim to be for a new social system. "Socialist" or "Labor" is just something left over in their names. They are simply capitalist parties, barely left of center.

* * *

During World War I, Lenin and others realized that social democracy had been a failure. Lenin wanted to begin Marxism again, reviving its revolutionary spirit. After his Bolsheviks took power in the Russian Empire, Lenin established the Communist International, aiming to build sections (parties) throughout the world. There were a famous 21 conditions for parties wishing to affiliate to the Communist International. One was to participate in elections. Lenin did not believe that elections to parliament could lead to a peaceful, legal, social change (not even in the U.S. or Britain!). But he thought that running for elections could provide opportunities to make revolutionary propaganda for the new Communist Parties. Serving in parliaments would be an even better platform for political propaganda. The Communist candidates would say, over and over again: *We need a revolution! Only a workers' revolution will solve our social problems!*

He also felt that there were times when the Communists could support a reformist party for election, while making vigorous criticisms. (This was at a time when the social democratic parties still claimed to be for socialism.) Communists should support the popular reformists in order to expose them for failing to live up to their socialist promises. He said the Communists would support the social democrats, "as a rope supports a hanged man."

Throughout the world, a large minority of revolutionary-minded activists were attracted to the Communist International--including many former anarchists. At first a majority of these new Communists disagreed with Lenin's desire to use elections. It is not often realized that Lenin (and fellow Bolsheviks such as Trotsky) were on the right of the early Communist movement. Lenin wrote a famous pamphlet against the Left Communists, *"Left-Wing" Communism--An Infantile Disorder* (in Lenin, 1971). In this debate, the issue of participating in parliament and elections was mixed up with other issues, whether to participate in existing labor unions (while opposing the unions' social democratic leaderships). Another issue, although not raised in this book, was whether to support national liberation struggles (while opposing the ideology of nationalism). These issues are not necessarily connected. I personally think that Lenin was right about participating in unions and supporting oppressed nations' right of self-determination against the imperialists--while wrong on electoralism. In any case, Lenin won the debate within the Communist International on all issues. Later some of the Left Communists were to split from the International, focusing on yet another issue. This was their opposition to the Russian Communists establishment of a one-party dictatorship (a party-state). Instead they championed the importance of the councils (soviets) as the basis of the workers' rule. They became known as the Council Communists.

The record of Communist Party electoralism is as dismal as that of the social democrats. The one difference is the manipulation of the CPs by the Stalinist Russian bureaucracy for its own foreign policy interests. Aside from that, the CPs were corrupted by the electoral process. A party can concentrate on a revolutionary message for a while, when it seems that revolution is right around the corner. But in a drawn-out peaceful period, the party leadership adapts. It has to offer practical reform proposals to satisfy its voters, if nothing else. Meanwhile, a layer of professional Communist politicians and officeholders developed. Now, with the final collapse of the Soviet Union, the Communist Parties have been free to come into their own. Every one of them has adopted a reform program of a so-called mixed economy (that is, the maintenance of capitalism). They are simply new social democrats.

Since Proudhon, there have been anarchists who have attempted to use electoral methods. Murray Bookchin is a prominent writer on anarchism, who has made many valuable contributions, especially on the integration of anarchist and ecological theories. However, he has also developed a program which he calls "Libertarian Municipalism" (Biehl, 1998; Bookchin, 1986a). A key part of his approach includes running in elections in towns and cities and trying to change municipal charters and laws. His goal is to change local communities into libertarian communist communes run by direct democracy. This is based on the belief that U.S. federalism still has life in it which could peacefully permit radical change without a revolution. It is associated with his arguments against a working class approach. Not surprisingly, his attempts to carry out Libertarian Municipalist electoralism have failed badly. Town and city governments are still part of the national and state governments, part of the overall state. Anything too radical on a local level will be overruled by higher levels of government or the courts. Local capitalists will withdraw from the community, destroying the local economy. The municipality would be put in receivership (the way New York State took over the budget process of New York City and of Yonkers with Financial Control Boards).

In short, all these electoralist approaches are attempts (in Marx's words of condemnation, cited at the beginning of the chapter), to "simply lay hold of the ready-made state machinery and wield it for [socialist] purposes." As revolutionary anarchists and others have expected, such methods have never worked. This does not mean that it is never useful to engage in voting (such as in referenda), or that there are never times when revolutionary anarchists might find it tactically useful to run in elections. It means that electoralism is mistaken as a strategy. (I have not been discussing the special U.S. situation, where many leftists have long supported the Democratic Party. This party has always been against socialism. It is the second party of U.S. capitalist imperialism, war waging, and racism. Any notion of supporting it is an abomination.)

*   *   *

Reformists have argued against anti-electoralism (and against opposition to alternative institutions as a strategy) that this leaves nothing to be done short of actual insurrections. It gives no way to fight for improvement in the daily lives of ordinary people, they have argued, until the people are ready for revolution.

In fact, *most improvements in the lives of working class and other oppressed people have come from nonelectoral struggles.* In the U.S., for example, in the thirties, workers asserted themselves through large and militant labor struggles, organizing the unemployed, forming unions, going on large-scale strikes, including factory occupations and mass picketing. Unionists violently fought company cops, vigilantes, regular police, and the National Guard. They *won* the right to form unions and to get benefits from the companies and the government. The weaknesses of today's unions are directly related to their abandonment of militant mass action in favor of lobbying. (Marx was virtually the first socialist thinker to take an unambiguously positive attitude toward unions--at a time when Proudhon was denouncing unions and strikes.)

The next wave of popular radicalization began in the late fifties and lasted through to the mid seventies (and is called, overall, the "sixties"). It began with the struggle against Jim Crow legal segregation by African-Americans in the U.S. South. This was opposed by mass, nonviolent, "civil disobedience" (which is another way to say lawbreaking). It was followed by urban "riots" (rebellions) in the North. As a result, legal segregation was defeated, the right of African-Americans to vote was won, anti-discrimination and affirmative action laws were gained.

Meanwhile a movement began against the evil U.S. war in Vietnam. Opposition to U.S. aggression included open draft refusal and informal draft dodging, mass demonstrations, campus occupations and strikes, a small amount of violence by protesters and a lot more by the authorities, soldiers going AWOL, soldiers mutinying, soldiers killing their officers ("fragging"). And, of course, the military pressure of the Vietnamese nationalists against the U.S. military and its stooges. Military conscription was ended even before the war was; finally the U.S. had to withdraw. We now know from secret presidential tapes, that President Nixon considered dropping atom bombs on North Vietnam but was afraid of its effect on the campuses. (He was right; we would have torn down the White House.)

Other rebellions of the time included the Gay, Lesbian, Bisexual, and Transgender Liberation movement. It began with a revolt in New York City at a bar on Christopher Street. Transvestites and Gay prostitutes (the least respected of the community) fought back against police harassment and sparked a national movement. Since then, the fight against the denial of resources for AIDS was waged through anarchistic direct action, by ACT-UP and others.

The Women's Liberation movement came out of the overall struggle, including many female activists with much experience in the antiracism and antiwar movements. Tired of being second class citizens in their own movements, they organized for equality. Demonstrations, conferences, and consciousness-raising groups played essential roles.

There was also an expansion of workers' struggles (something often ignored in looking at the period). There was a wave of wildcat strikes in key industries, usually led by Black workers, most famously a national postal strike. Unions were successfully built in government employment and in health care, again especially including Black workers. It is often forgotten that M.L. King was assassinated when he was in Memphis to give support to a union struggle by African-American sanitation workers.

Of course, legal and elective activities played their parts in these struggles. The politicians would run around to get in front of the angry people and then claim to be the leaders. Eventually these treacherous methods worked, resulting in the decay of the movements.

The revolutionary program of smashing the state and dismantling capitalism, then, is not just a long-range goal. The more that mass struggles are extreme, militant, disrespectful of authority, disreputable, and angry--that is, revolutionary--the more the ruling class is likely to grant reforms (when it can). The rulers must be taught to fear the working class. A nice, housebroken, and legal, opposition does not pressure them; it can be ignored. So can a small group of revolutionaries. But a large movement which is also radical can win gains when nothing else will.

*　*　*

There is a last reason why the working class should be revolutionary. Workers, it is said by their enemies, have many weaknesses. They show widespread racism, sexism, superpatriotism, religious fundamentalism, contempt for those of lower status and admiration for those who do better, a mostly hopeless desire to rise into the upper class, and a general desire for strong leaders to save them. There is a lot of truth in these stereotypes. There is no evidence, however, that workers are *more* likely to be racist, sexist, superpatriotic, etc. than *other* classes. The question remains, how will the working class overcome these weaknesses? Through struggle against their real enemies.

"How does a people or a class become fit to rule in their own name? *Only by fighting to do so.....*Only by fighting for democratic power do they educate themselves and raise themselves up to the level of being able to wield that power. There has never been any other way for any class." (Draper,1992, p. 33; emphasis Draper's)

Chapter 4. The Marxist Transitional State

"Between capitalist and communist society there is a period of revolutionary transformation from one to the other. There is a corresponding period of transition in the political sphere and in this period the state can only take the form of a *revolutionary dictatorship of the proletariat*." So wrote Marx in his *Critique of the Gotha Program* (1974b, p. 355; Marx's emphasis).

This leads to the common interpretation of Marx as advocating the smashing of the capitalist state, then the building a new, workers' state, a dictatorship no less. Eventually this dictatorial state should somehow "wither away" (sometimes referred to as "dying out"). This concept is counterposed to that of the anarchists, who are supposed to want to leap immediately from the capitalist state into a classless, stateless, moneyless, defenseless, communist society.

There is truth in these concepts of the Marxist and anarchist views. But they do not cover the whole truth. In particular, there is a libertarian interpretation of Marx which is fairly close to the real views of many anarchists.

The notion of a transitional political stage between capitalism and a fully socialist (communist) system seems almost "common sense." During and for a while after a revolution, there will continue to be a need to defend the new society from counterrevolutionary armies and from conspiracies for sabotage. Whatever the case eventually, for a time there will continue to be a large number of psychopaths and antisocial actors, people raised in the loveless society of capitalism, people who need to be prevented from harming others. All of which suggests the need for some sort of state-like organization to provide armed defense and security. Meanwhile the mass of people will have been raised under capitalism. They will respond to the incentives of idealism offered by the new system, but may need to be also motivated by material incentives to keep them working. This suggests something short of fully-realized communism. (Marx distinguished between the lower stage of communism and a higher, completed, phase.)

Even the concept of the eventual withering away (dying out) of the state has a certain sense to it. On the one hand, as time goes by, the defeated capitalist class will decrease in size and influence and will gradually be reconciled to the new society. The old ones will die out and their children will be assimilated. There will no longer be a need to hold down the bourgeoisie. As the revolution spreads internationally and various civil wars are won, there will cease to be a need for any kind of armies. In a prosperous, healthy, and happy society, the extent of antisocial behavior will drastically decrease. The need for police-type controls will also drastically decrease. On the other hand, there will be more and more participation by the working people in the management of society. People will be more educated. They will have more leisure time to participate. As everyone joins in *governing*, there ceases to be a (separate) *government*. In all previous revolutions, the people participated in the mass uprisings, but then returned to their daily grind while a few became the new rulers. Now, with the productivity of current technology combined with a socialist social system, people will have more free time--popular participation can keep on increasing after the initial revolution.

However, empirically the concepts of the transitional stage, the transitional workers state, the withering away of the state, etc., have not faired so well. Far from withering away, the states established by Marxists--beginning with Lenin's Soviet Union--did not wither away but developed into ugly totalitarianisms. After 75 years of totalitarian state capitalism, the state of the Soviet Union came apart--not the same as withering away--while the state of Communist China still goes on, even with a privatized economy.

The theory of a transitional state and economy served to ideologically justify the 75 years of despotism, not only for the paid mouthpieces of state Communism but also for its Marxist critics. Those who did not see the USSR as a workers' socialist paradise, at least thought of it as a degenerated workers' state, a postcapitalist society, or a society on the road to socialism. All these theorists agreed that the Soviet Union (actually a capitalist and imperialist state) was somehow different from, and better than, the capitalist West and therefore to be supported against it. They took its side in the Cold War.

* * *

Marx advocated the "dictatorship of the proletariat." What he meant was that there would be a time after the overthrow of the capitalist state when the working class, as a whole class, would rule over the capitalists and their hangers-on. It was not at all counterposed to the democratic self-organization of the working class (just as the dictatorship of the bourgeoisie over the workers is consistent with bourgeois democracy).

What Marx and the Marxists meant by the term "dictatorship of the proletariat" is discussed by Draper (1987; see also Ehrenberg, 1992). Draper demonstrates that Marx and Engels meant the democratic rule of the workers as a class. He also shows that--with one exception-- every other Marxist from their time to that of Lenin and Trotsky, and after, interpreted it to mean repressive rule, usually by a minority. This was the interpretation both of those reformists who opposed the term and the Leninists who accepted it. The single exception was Rosa Luxemburg, who used the term to mean the workers' democratic class rule. Luxemburg has been a major influence on libertarian Marxists.

The so-called dictatorship of the proletariat--in Marx's classical conception--was to be different from all previous class dictatorships in certain ways. It would not be the rule of a minority class over the majority of the population. It would be the rule of the big majority (the workers plus other oppressed classes, such as the peasants, who would follow the workers' lead) over a minority (the capitalists). It would not aim to keep a ruling (dictating) class in power, but would aim to dissolve all classes into a classless, stateless, socialism. Because of these differences I think that it is not useful to describe the rule of the workers as a dictatorship, whatever Marx once meant by it. This is aside from the fact that the word has changed over time and is virtually never used to mean class rule anymore. Few people today would use dictatorship as consistent with democracy. And of course, the Communist governments have used "dictatorship of the proletariat" to mean the dictatorial rule of the Communist Party *over* the proletariat.

* * *

As we have seen, ancient slave owning governments and modern capitalist governments could take many forms, democratic or tyrannical. Many Marxists have argued that the same is true of working class rule. That is, the workers could rule through the most democratic, Commune-like, system of workers' councils, but they might also rule through the domination of a minority revolutionary party (as under Lenin) or of one-man totalitarianism (such as Stalin). These are supposedly all forms of "the dictatorship of the proletariat." Such an argument was used by those who, unlike Communist Party members, recognized that Soviet Russia was far from democratic, but still supported it as somehow socialist or a workers' state (such as Leon Trotsky or Isaac Deutscher).

However, the working class is different from the slaveowners or the capitalists. It has no private property in industry. It does not own slaves nor stocks in corporations, to be protected by various forms of government. The proletariat can only manage society collectively, cooperatively, and democratically. Modern technological society is more and more collectivized. The collectivity of industry is not, in itself, socialist. Capitalism collectivizes in its big, semi-monopolistic, corporations. Stalinist state-capitalism was collectivized. The question is, Who controls ("owns") the collectivized economy? Traditional capitalists? State bureaucrats? Or the working class as a whole? If someone runs the economy (and state), presumably "for" the workers, then the workers are still where they have always been, on the bottom, taking orders from bosses, being exploited. If the workers are to turn society onto the path of abolishing the state, classes, and all forms of domination, then they themselves must manage society. The working class must be democratic or it cannot be free. (Of course, the forms of working class self-management may vary widely, so long as they are democratic.)

*   *   *

Marx's final vision of what would follow a revolution--in the transitional stage--was formed by what he learned from the working people of the Paris Commune of spring 1871. There has been much written on the Paris Commune; I will briefly summarize. In 1870 a war broke out between the French dictatorship of Louis Napoleon and the German empire led by Chancellor Otto von Bismarck. The Prussian military machine crushed the French army and captured Emperor Napoleon. A conservative batch of French politicians declared for a republic and prepared to negotiate a capitulation to the Germans who had by now occupied much of France. Eventually they held elections for a parliament, which was dominated by reactionary, monarchist, politicians from the rural provinces. However, the working people of Paris would not surrender to the German invaders. The Parisian workers were armed, in the form of a volunteer National Guard which had its own cannon and other arms. The French bourgeoisie feared the armed, self-organized, Parisian workers more than they feared the German occupiers (who, after all, still represented a capitalist class). Civil war broke out in France, between the capitalist state and the working people of Paris. The Parisians seized power and declared the city a "commune," after the Paris Commune of the great French revolution. Eventually the capitalist government, with help from the Germans, defeated the Parisian workers. It went on a bloody rampage, murdering tens of thousands of workers and imprisoning many thousands more.

But for 72 days the Paris Commune stood. Marx was impressed by what it did and by what it might have done, that is, the tendencies which he saw in it and the promise that they made of a different future. In *The Civil War in France* (Marx & Engels 1971), he described its radically democratic measures: replacing the bureaucrats by officials elected by the neighborhood sections, who could be easily recalled by the voters, and who did not get paid more than most workers. No elected officials to be paid more than workers' wages. The standing permanent army was replaced by a popular militia, the National Guard. Police were no longer appointed from above but were controlled by the people of the sections. There was no executive branch separate from the legislative. Had there been time, every local village, town, and city would have been run by such an ultra-democratic system, with delegates of each locality sent to regionally central cities, and then delegates from each region sent to Paris to form a national coordinating body.

Economically, regulations were passed to benefit the workers and poor of Paris, such as ending night work for bakers and canceling debts. Factories and workplaces which had been abandoned by the capitalists were turned over to the workers to run. There was a general desire to promote worker-run cooperatives, although there was little time to achieve much.

Marx summarized the antistate measures of the Paris Commune most clearly in the first outline he wrote for his essay, "It was a revolution against the *State* itself..., a resumption by the people for the people of its own social life. It was not a revolution to transfer it from one faction of the ruling classes to the other, but a revolution to break down this horrid machinery of class domination itself" (Marx & Engels,1971, p. 152; Marx's emphasis).

Anarchists agreed with Marx about the 1871 Commune and even accused him of stealing his antistatist interpretation from them (unlikely). Bakunin hailed the Paris Commune as "a bold, clearly formulated negation of the state" (Bakunin, 1980, p. 264).

Reviewing what Marx had written about the Paris Commune, Engels made two apparently contradictory comments. In 1891, he challenged "the Social-Democratic philistine" to "Look at the Paris Commune. That was the Dictatorship of the Proletariat" (in Marx & Engels, 1971, p. 34). He was both challenging the growing right-wing of the German Social Democratic Party to face the revolutionary perspective of the rule of the working class, and he was identifying that rule ("dictatorship") with the radical democracy of the Commune.

Yet, in 1875 Engels had written a letter proposing changes in the party program based on the experience of the Paris Commune. "The whole talk about the state should be dropped, especially since the Commune, which was no longer a state in the proper sense of the word....We would therefore propose replacing *state* everywhere by *Gemeinwesen* [community], a good old German word which can very well take the place of the French word *commune*" (quoted in Lenin, 1970b, p. 333). After quoting this, Lenin commented, "What a howl about 'anarchism' would be raised by the leading lights of present-day 'Marxism'...if such an amendment of the program were suggested to them" (same)!

So, to Engels the Paris Commune was both "the dictatorship of the proletariat" (that is, the rule of the working class) and, at the same time, "no longer a state in the proper sense of the word." It was not a state because it was no longer a social organization separate from the workers and above them. It was the democratic self-organization of the workers themselves. It was no longer a minority controlling an exploited majority but the majority controlling the formerly-exploiting minority--and therefore no longer a state.

The same dual point is made by Paul Mattick, a Council Communist (anti-Leninist Marxist), writing that, for "Marx and Engels...the victorious working class would neither institute a new state nor seize control of the existing state, but exercise its dictatorship.... Although assuming functions previously associated with those of the state, this [working class] dictatorship is not to become a new state....It is not through the state that socialism can be realized, as this would exclude the self-determination of the working class, which is the essence of socialism" (1983. pp. 160-161). This is an important point, that even from a Marxist perspective, *there is no such thing as a workers' state.*

* * *

Lenin's book, *State and Revolution* (1970b), is well-known to be his most libertarian work. It is mainly an interpretation of almost everything Marx and Engels wrote about the state. Lenin wrote it under the influence of the deepening Russian revolution, where the soviets (councils) raised the possibility of repeating the experience of the Paris Commune on a larger scale. This was before he had actually taken power and the revolution had turned authoritarian. Here Lenin repeatedly denounced the leading Marxists for criticizing the anarchists for (what Lenin regarded as) the wrong reasons, namely for calling for smashing the bourgeois state and for their goal of a stateless society.

Instead, Lenin wrote, "What withers away after the revolution is the proletarian *state or semi-state*" (1970b, p. 298; my emphasis). "...According to Marx, the proletariat needs only a state which is withering away, i.e., a state so constituted that *it begins to wither away immediately...*" (1970b, p. 303; my emphasis). "...Democracy, introduced as fully and consistently as is at all conceivable, is transformed from bourgeois into proletarian democracy; from the state (= a special force for the suppression of a particular class) into *something which is no longer the state proper*" (1970, p. 317; my emphasis). "The Commune *was ceasing* to be a state..." (1970, p. 334; Lenin's emphasis). "...During the *transition*...the 'state' is *still* necessary, but this is now a transitional state. It is no longer a state in the proper sense of the word..." (1970, p.352; Lenin's emphasis).

Lenin thought that the achievement of a completely stateless society might take a long time. But he believed that the process would *begin immediately* after the revolution. Immediately the big majority of working people would participate in running society and in holding down the former ruling class. In fact, the program of Lenin's Bolshevik Party, before the revolution, was for "All Power to the Soviets"; workers' control of industry; women's committees to distribute consumer goods; peasant councils to distribute the land of the landlords, etc., apparently consistent with this antistatist perspective. The Russian anarchists generally felt that the Bolsheviks' program was at least friendly to anarchist values. They allied with the Leninists during the revolution.

* * *

Apparently *Marx's and Engels' approach to the dictatorship of the proletariat and the transitional state can be interpreted in a libertarian, antistatist, fashion.* It has been so interpreted by the Council Communists as well as by Lenin at one point. Yet this libertarian interpretation of Marxism is contradictory to the totalitarian states developed by the Marxists, including Lenin. This is a paradox. In fact, Marx's *Civil War in France* and Lenin's *State and Revolution* have been widely read by supporters of the Stalinist dictatorships. How could they read them and still support state capitalism? There are several reasons .

Statements by Marx, Engels, and Lenin are contradictory. It is not clear to what extent the antiauthoritarian interpretation is really correct. In *State and Revolution*, Lenin, as mentioned, said that the workers' state would immediately begin to wither away, but that he could not say if it ever would be completely gone. So, even in his most libertarian work, he said that the state might exist indefinitely. Engels, in his 1891 introduction to *The Civil War in France*, modified his position that the Paris Commune implied an *immediate* end to the state: "...The state is...at best an evil inherited by the proletariat after its victorious struggle for class supremacy, whose worst sides the victorious proletariat, just like the Commune, cannot avoid having to lop off at once as much as possible until such time as a generation reared in new, free, social conditions is able to throw the entire lumber of the state on the scrap heap" (in Marx & Engels, 1971, p.34). In this conception, the state now *is* the dictatorship of the proletariat. The revolution could only "lop off" some of the "worst sides", while the state itself would last for one or more generations!

Furthermore, there is a problem in the very concept of the "withering away of the state" (Tabor 1988). It is consistent with Marxism's tendency to see history as automatically moving along, from slavery to feudalism to capitalism, then automatically generating class consciousness in the working class, and inevitably culminating in socialism. This tendency goes back to Marx and is probably derived from Hegel with his dialectical view of history moving toward an inevitable end (namely Hegel's philosophy and the Prussian monarchy). This tendency in Marxism denies choice, will, and the moral vision necessary for a socialist revolution. (I do not say that this is the only tendency in Marx's Marxism, but it is a major one and it became dominant in both social democratic and Stalinist versions of Marxism.)

Would the workers' state (or semi-state) really wither away automatically? Would not there be tendencies for the state-like features to consolidate themselves? Might not a layer of officials develop around the institution which would become a new ruling class? Might not the need to resist the old ruling class cause the military and police features of the semi-state to become more authoritarian, more statist?

According to the Marxist formula, revolutionary activists should spend all their efforts in creating a new state. The withering away of the new state should be left to happen on its own. But if all your efforts are to make a state, then what you are likely to end up with is...a state. The alternative is for the withering away to also be something to be done. The new semi-state (or whatever) is to *be withered*. Granting that certain state-like functions need to be created (e.g. military defense against counterrevolutionary armies), there needs to be a conscious effort--a plan--to fight against the consolidation of a new state. There needs to be a constant and deliberate effort to counteract statist tendencies, to keep them within necessary bounds, and to move in a stateless direction. The rule should be, *as much voluntary self-management as possible, with only as much repression and centralization (semi-statism) as is absolutely necessary at the time.*

* * *

One way to check statist tendencies is to maintain a multiparty, multi-tendency, democracy in the new councils--that is, to permit *freedom of political association*, political pluralism. Before, during, and after a revolution there is going to be a wide variety of political views, even among revolutionary workers. A major reason for forming a revolutionary anarchist organization is to fight against the authoritarian parties--from the social democrats to the Leninists. Anarchists need to organize to persuade the workers to rely on themselves instead of new bosses. However, an anarchist organization will not exist only to oppose other organizations (the parties which seek power). It also exists to work with other political tendencies. North America, for example, is a large and complex society. It is unlikely that one political organization will have all the right answers and will attract all the best militants. There will be a need to ally with all those organizations moving in the direction of workers' democracy.

There are two different types of political organizations. There are, first, relatively narrow, programmatic, "party"-like, organizations. These are voluntary associations formed around a program, and have a fairly high level of agreement among their members about the program. They use words and actions to persuade other people of their program. On the other hand, there are mass, broad, organizations such as unions, community associations, African-American rights organizations, or workers' councils. These include a wide variety of people and have minimal requirements to join. For example, to join a union, people have to work for that boss or work in that trade. Outside of this, they are likely to disagree on all sorts of things such as politics or religion (although management personnel may not join, which is what makes unions, for all their limitations, class institutions). It is important not to confuse the two sorts of organizations. Stalinists deliberately treat their narrow political organization as though it represents the whole of the heterogeneous working class, for example. Some anarchists make the reciprocal mistake of aiming to dissolve themselves into the mass organizations and ignore the need to fight to persuade people of their revolutionary politics. (It may sound strange to some people to hear such discussions about types of organization from an anarchist, since there is the widespread mistaken view that anarchists are against organization.)

There is nothing in Marx's writings about the value of multi-tendency democracy under socialism, although (to be fair) he may have taken it for granted. Marxists following him developed the concept that there was only one party which would represent the true interests of the workers, which is at least consistent with Marx's concept that only his ideas represented the workers. Lenin was certain that his party was the only party with genuine working class consciousness, whatever the consciousness of actual workers. It is well known that his *State and Revolution* says nothing about the role of the party or parties--a peculiar omission for someone who spent his life developing a party. He may have assumed that the party would be there behind the scenes or that the party would have itself withered away. In either case he had no conception of a multiparty democracy. As the Russian revolution developed, one opposition party after another was outlawed, for good or bad reasons. The anarchists were suppressed. Even if we assume, for the sake of argument, that each suppression was necessary during the revolution, the Leninists may be said to have made a virtue out of "necessity." One Communist leader quipped that under Communism there was room for many parties, one in power and the others in jail. (Anarchists also did not explicitly advocate multi-tendency democracy, but their program was for the freedom to organize voluntary associations.)

As we will see, the Russian revolution was not made by the Bolsheviks alone but by an alliance of the Leninists with others, including anarchists. The falling apart of that united front--its replacement with a one-party dictatorship-- was a major milestone in the degeneration of the revolution.

Eventually the parties may indeed wither away, while new issues and ways of organizing develop. Some local communities may use consensus-based decision-making. The united front of revolutionary organizations may be a step on that road. Different regions may organize their politics in various ways. However, anarchism will never create a perfectly harmonious society. People will have conflicting interests or concerns, different ideas, alternate desires. They will always need to be free to get together with like-minded people to express their opinions and try to persuade others.

* * *

Perhaps the key to Marxism's tendency to totalitarianism is its centralism. From Marx to Lenin, Marxists have emphasized the need for centralized economic and political institutions, that is, that power be focused on a center, where one or a few people make decisions.

For Marx there were both political and economic determinants of this centralism. Politically, as a leading revolutionary democrat in Germany, he opposed all the chaotic minor kingdoms which broke up the country. He called for a unified Germany run from a national center by an elected parliament. This would overthrow the local aristocrats as well as create a national internal market so that capitalism would be free to develop the economy. He was following the tradition of centralist radical democracy identified with French Jacobinism. (This is different from the U.S., where the radical Jeffersonian democrats were for a decentralized federation and the conservative Hamiltonians were for a centralized near-monarchy. Of course Jefferson's radical democracy was for white people only.)

After the failure of the European revolutions of 1848, Marx and Engels wrote an *Address of the Central Committee to the Communist League* (written in March 1850). In this they denounced the bourgeois democrats for advocating a "federated republic" and declared, "...the workers must not only strive for the one and indivisible republic, but also...for the most decisive centralization of power in the hands of the state authority" (Marx,1974b, p. 328). They referred to the example of the French revolutionaries who fought for centralization.

But in 1885--that is, after the Paris Commune--Engels wrote a footnote, "...This passage is based on a misunderstanding.... It is now known that during the entire [1791 French] revolution...the whole administration of the departments, districts, and municipalities consisted of authorities elected by the local population, and that the authorities acted with complete freedom within the limits of the general state legislation. This provincial and local self-government, resembling the American, indeed became the strongest instrument of the revolution....[This] does not contradict political and national centralization..." (in Marx,1974b, p. 329). He noted that it was Napoleon who destroyed this local self-government, replacing it with a topdown system of appointees. His last sentence is ambiguous, to me anyway. Did he mean that federalism does not necessarily contradict national unification (true), or did he mean that strict centralization is somehow still compatible with local self-rule? I do not know. However, he rarely referred to the question and it did not affect Marxist theory thereafter.

Marx's writing on the Paris Commune have often been cited on this topic. Eduard Bernstein, the "Revisionist" (openly reformist) Marxist, claimed that Marx's writings here were similar to that of the anarchist/decentralist Proudhon--in order to attack Marx. Lenin responded by indignantly denying this and insisting that Marx remained a centralist. Actually Marx did not address the issue of centralism/decentralism in these writings. His work on the Paris Commune was certainly consistent with a decentralist perspective, but it is unclear whether he drew this conclusion. Engels and he criticized the Commune for not acting quickly and decisively to attack the reactionary forces when they were in disarray, and for not seizing the gold of the Bank of France. Lenin and others cited this as evidence that Marx wanted the Commune to be more centralized and dictatorial--which does not follow.

However, unlike some anarchists, Marx did not discuss the efforts to revive the neighborhood assemblies in Paris which had played such an important role in the 18th century French revolution. Nor did he discuss the important role of local clubs in the Paris Commune. More generally, *Marx and Engels never raised the importance of local, direct, face-to-face, democracy.* Their discussion of working class democracy is always about elected officials who can be controlled by the ranks, the most democratic form of representative democracy. But they never wrote about rooting it in the daily control by workers of their institutions and communities. Apparently this never occurred to them.

* * *

Finally, his writings on the Commune say nothing about Marx's belief in economic and technological centralization. Marx and Engels were greatly influenced by the big factories and big companies of capitalism. They saw this as technological progress. The big factories led to big productivity and big cities with big, concentrated, masses of proletarians. These big forces would lead to socialist revolution. This is the message of *Capital*. Socialism would build on this and produce an even bigger industry. Of course Marx was aware that big businesses were created in order to better control the workers, and that the "concentration and centralization of capital" was often done for financial reasons rather than for increased productivity. However, he believed that these factors served the long term interest of improved technology and productivity through big industry.

In *The Communist Manifesto*, Marx and Engels raised a socialist program, based on this belief in the value of centralization. "The proletariat will use its political supremacy, to wrest by degrees, all capital from the bourgeoisie, to centralize all instruments of production in the hands of the state..." (in Draper, 1998, p. 155). This was followed by a ten point program, which included, "5. Centralization of credit in the hands of the state....6. Centralization of the means of communication and transport in the hands of the state. 7. Extension of factories and instruments of production owned by the state....8. Equal liability of all to labor. Establishment of industrial armies..." (same). The 1850 *Address to the Communist League* also raised the demand for government ownership and centralization. Whatever other changes they made in their program, Marx and Engels never gave up this goal of a completely centralized economy.

Not that Marx and Engels were worshipers of the state. On the contrary, they ended this section of the *Manifesto* by declaring that once the national economy is centralized and statified, the state will cease to exist *as a state*. "When...class distinctions have disappeared, and all production has been concentrated in the hands of a vast association of the whole nation, the public power will lose its political character" (in Draper, 1998, p. 157).

Unfortunately, even though it may no longer be called a state, that "vast association of the whole nation," which has concentrated all production in its hands, sounds pretty state-like, in the sense of being a centralized bureaucratic machine above the rest of society. The members of those industrial armies, who are "liable" (forced) to labor, may not think that they have common interests with the central planners. There may have to be a revival of police forces or the military to keep the workers from rebelling. In short, this public power would regain its "political" (that is, statist) nature.

This is even more true of Lenin, who always insisted that he was a "centralist." Even when he supported federalism (as in the federal joining of separate nations), he saw this as a temporary measure, on the road to complete centralization. His party and state were supposedly run on the principle of "democratic centralism."

In *State and Revolution*, along with the apparently libertarian passages, Lenin makes clear his belief in centralist economics. His model, he says, is the wartime "state-monopoly capitalism" of modern imperialism, especially of the German state. He admires the German post-office and all sorts of centralized massive enterprises which merge government and capitalist aspects. If only, he says, the imperialist-capitalist state is replaced by a state of the working class, to run the same sort of centralized enterprises, then this would be the next step toward socialism. Under these conditions, "*All* citizens are transformed into hired employees of the state....*All* citizens become employees and workers of a *single* countrywide state 'syndicate.'...The whole of society will become a single office and a single factory..." (1970b, p. 360-361; Lenin's emphasis). For a period he expected there to still be "technicians, foremen, and accountants" (p. 323) and other officials in this one big factory. The state capitalist aspects of this vision do not really need to be elaborated. The whole society as one enormous factory or office with foremen and officials! Under the pressure of the failure of the revolution to spread, foreign invasions and civil wars, and the extreme poverty of the country, such concepts overwhelmed the libertarian aspects of Lenin's vision and produced a totalitarian nightmare.

In comparison to the Marxist program, Kropotkin wrote (in an article on anarchism for the 1910 *Encyclopedia Britannica*), "The anarchists consider...that to hand over to the state all the main sources of economic life--the land, the mines, the railways, banking, insurance, and so on--as also the management of all the main branches of industry, in addition to all the functions already accumulated in its hands (education, state-supported religions, defense of the territory, etc.) would mean to create a new instrument of tyranny. State capitalism would only increase the powers of bureaucracy and capitalism" (1975, pp. 109-110). With the benefit of over a century of hindsight, it is clear who was right.

CHAPTER 5. ANARCHIST ALTERNATIVES TO THE STATE

Of the tasks presently carried out by the state, at least three will still be needed, at least for a period during and after a revolution. They are the military defense of the territory, dealing with "criminal" antisocial behavior, and the overall coordination of society. How might anarchism handle these tasks--without a state?

In the above encyclopedia article, Kropotkin wrote that, under anarchism, "...voluntary associations...would...substitute themselves for the state in all its functions. They would represent an interwoven network, composed of an infinite variety of groups and federations of all sizes and degrees, local, regional, national, and international-- temporary or more or less permanent--for all possible purposes: production, consumption, and exchange, communications, sanitary arrangements, education, *mutual protection, defense of the territory*, and so on..." (1975, p. 108; my emphasis). The associations would make agreements with each other. They would develop in the direction of increased decentralization and local initiative. They would replace capitalism by socialist cooperation and nonprofit production.

Kropotkin did not expect an immediate leap into a peaceful world. For a while, certain functions carried out by the state would still be needed. Under anarchism, there would be associations for "mutual protection [and] defense of the territory." Revolutionary anarchists have always agreed on the need for armed forces during a revolution.

Instead of a regular, state-run, army, they have advocated the voluntary arming of the people, and the creation of a workers' militia, possibly using guerilla tactics. Such forces should be coordinated and supervised by workers' councils. (Today the term "militia" has become used to describe any nongovernment armed force, including right-wing bands or armed groups organized by jihadists in Iraq. I am using it in the traditional sense of an armed people.)

Anarchists have organized military forces--very effective ones too. During the Russian revolution, the anarchist Nestor Makno organized a guerilla army of peasants in Ukraine. It beat back several counterrevolutionary ("White") armies and was only defeated, finally, by Trotsky's "Red" army through treachery. During the Spanish revolution/ civil war of 1936, the fascist forces were beaten back at first by the formation of anarchist columns, the most famous being led by Benvenuto Durruti. Zapata's army in Mexico may be seen as a parallel example of a libertarian military force.

Anarchism will replace the current standing or regular armed forces, an agency of the ruling class, with a democratic, self-armed people. This is a concept which goes back for ages, to tribal democracies. In the direct democracy of ancient Athens, the (male) citizens were the soldiers. If they voted for war in the Assembly, then the citizens went home and took out their armor and weapons. Unlike today, they did not vote to send *someone else* to fight. The philosopher Rousseau admired the ancient Greeks, as well as the Swiss of his more recent time who had a similar system of direct democracy and armed citizenry. He felt that the rise of professional soldiers went together with the rise of government by professional "representatives"; the people became enslaved as they ceased to participate in the essential tasks of government (Roberts, 1976).

In the American revolution, the professional British imperial army was defeated by a ragtag force, half a volunteer regular army (never very professional) and half militia. Disliking a professional, regular army so much, the revolutionaries wrote phrases saying, "Standing armies are dangerous to liberty and ought not to be kept," into the constitutions of

Pennsylvania, Delaware, Massachusetts, North Carolina, and Maryland (Hart, 1998). They wrote into the Constitution's Bill of Rights, Article two, that citizens should have the right to "keep and bear arms" in order to maintain "a well-regulated militia" which is "necessary to the security of a free state." This Article has become a stumbling block for statist liberals, who want only the police and military (and criminals?) to have guns, and it has been championed by the Right--which has, however, no intention of disbanding the army in favor of a militia!

As the capitalist democrats abandoned the slogan of the militia, it entered the socialist tradition. From the Paris Commune, both Marx and the anarchists drew the lesson that peoples could be defended by a nation in arms instead of a regular, professional, army. Marx declared, "The first decree of the Commune...was the suppression of the standing army, and substitution for it of the armed people" (Marx, 1971, p. 71). Bebel, a founder of the German Marxist party, campaigned for a militia in place of the standing Imperial army. In the period before the First World War, Jean Jaures, a prominent French reformist social democrat, wrote the influential *The New Army*. Motivated in part by a hatred of the reactionary French officer corps (this was after the Dreyfus Affair), he proposed replacing it with a territorial militia system, purely defensive in character, using conscription. As a reformist, he proposed it for capitalist society, to be carried out by a liberal government.

Similarly, the idea of a workers' militia was championed by the revolutionary wing of Marxism. Lenin particularly raised it in counterposition to liberal proposals for international arbitration or disarmament, which he regarded as spreading illusions in the imperialist states. As the Russian revolution began to break out, he raised demands that capitalists be forced to pay for training their workers in weaponry, that the police be replaced by workers' patrols, and that military officers be elected. Volunteer groups of workers, organized as Red Guards, and various guerilla forces, played an important part in the first stage of the Communist seizure of power.

However, the Communists did not organize a democratic or militia-based army. With Leon Trotsky as the top commander, they built a centralized, professional-type of Red Army, based on conscription, and using the services of tens of thousands of officers from the old czarist army (Deutscher 1954). The Communists claimed that this departure from their ideals was necessary for various objective reasons--mainly the backwardness and ignorance of the country. True or not, Nestor Makhno and other anarchists organized a guerrilla army in the Ukraine, despite similar circumstances . As mentioned, he Makhnoites successfully beat off a couple of rightist armies and held off the Red Army for years.

During World War II, an important if subordinate role was played by guerrilla forces. This included the maquis of the French resistance, the Italian partisans, the guerrilla struggle in Eastern Europe, particularly in Yugoslavia, Albania, and Greece, the partisan forces in Russia and Ukraine, and the anti-Japanese guerrilla wars throughout China, southeast Asia, and the islands. (As the name implies, guerrilla war goes back at least to the Spanish struggle against Napoleon's invasion.)

After the world war, guerrilla war played a major part in the Communist revolutions in China, Yugoslavia, Albania, and Cuba-- all of whom showed independence from the Soviet Union, unlike the Communist governments which had been installed by the Russian army. Guerrilla tactics were also part of the Algerian war of independence from France. The Vietnamese war against the Japanese, French, and finally the U.S. was fought on a guerrilla basis to a great extent. The fight against, and eventual defeat of, the U.S. army by the Vietnamese was a major factor in the 'sixties worldwide radicalization. Belief in a guerrilla strategy became an article of faith on the Left.

Guerrilla methods were not limited to the Left. In Afghanistan, guerrilla warriors, who were often Islamic fundamentalists, drove out the Russian army. This played a major role in the final collapse of the Soviet Union. Guerrilla methods are being used against the U.S. right now in Iraq by nationalist and Islamicist resistance fighters.

Several countries have made militia or guerrilla methods an essential part of their defense plans. Switzerland had never ceased to have a militia system, from the Middle Ages to today (Roberts, 1976). A large part of the male population is in the army on a part-time basis. By law, male citizens are required to keep a rifle or machine gun at home (making the Swiss the most highly armed population in the world, although with a low crime rate). There are few professional military people. Interestingly, Israel was influenced by the Swiss system when it set up its own military structure. As a colonial-settler state, Israel cannot afford a large standing army, but needs to be able to rapidly mobilize its small population for war in a crisis. The Israelis use an armed population, a large reserve force, weaponry and munitions scattered in regional centers, not for a decentralized defense but for a rapid call-up system (given its small size, it is not hard to move mobilized forces from their call-up locations to wherever needed).

Another country which built guerrilla methods into its defense program was Yugoslavia (Roberts, 1976). A system of popular defense existed alongside of , and coequal to, the regular army. It had a local reserve system which could be rapidly mobilized to form a defense in depth or shift to guerrilla tactics. The constitution specifically forbade surrender under any circumstances. (The widespread availability of weapons was a factor in the bloodiness of the wars which tore Yugoslavia apart after Tito's death.) Other countries, such as Sweden and North Korea have included such methods in their defense plans.

A militia is a form of popular armed forces. It is often advocated together with the method of *territorial defense* or *defense in depth*. These imply an approach of defending the country foot by foot, making the enemy pay for every advance. However, as Israel shows, it can also be used as a National Guard-type of reserves, for rapid mobilization. *Guerrilla* techniques imply hit-and-run tactics, to wear down the enemy by attrition. However, local militia forces can turn into guerrillas. Guerrilla units can merge to form larger forces for regular set battles (as they did in China and Vietnam). Large regular armies can break up into guerrilla (*partisan*) forces. Regular armies can use small elite units for guerrilla-like *commando* tactics. *An armed nation of citizen soldiers can be very flexible in its forms of fighting.* (The issue of conscription versus volunteer recruiting of the military is separate from the form of the armed forces.)

In the late 'seventies and early 'eighties, some European peace activists began to raise the question whether it would be possible to defend Western Europe from the Soviet Union without nuclear weapons or U.S. forces. It was obvious that even a "limited" nuclear war fought over Europe would destroy the subcontinent. Even a conventional, nonnuclear, regular war would leave a smoking ruin. They consulted with liberal military experts, reviewed the history of guerrilla wars, and examined the defense plans of Yugoslavia, Switzerland, and Sweden. They came up with several proposals relevant to my topic (Alternate Defense Commission, 1983; Barnaby & Boeker, 1982; Mackay & Fernbach, 1983; Roberts, 1976; Smith, 1982).

What they proposed, in general, was a non-nuclear defense program for Western Europe with a military structure and armaments program which obviously emphasized defense rather than offensive capacity, in order to be clearly non-threatening to other countries. They proposed limiting regular armed forces to the role of protecting borders, so that any invader would be forced to pay a price and militias would have time to mobilize. The population would be organized in a militia, with widespread military training, repeated over the years, and with local weapons depots and bunkers scattered throughout the countryside. Weapons could include not just pistols and rifles but also Stingers and similar precision-guided missiles. One or two soldiers can carry and use them against tanks and airplanes. Either a defense in depth or guerrilla tactics could be planned for, depending on various conditions, such as the terrain. Urban guerrilla tactics are also mentioned, including assassination and sabotage. Also methods of unarmed civilian resistance would be taken from proposals for nonviolent methods (King-Hall, 1960; Roberts et al, 1964). These include strikes, go-slows, and other forms of noncooperation, and peaceful demonstrations and propaganda directed at the invader's troops.

The idea of changing the U.S. military into one modeled on the Swiss or Israeli citizen soldier system was raised by Gary Hart (1998). He had been a presidential candidate, a Democratic senator from Colorado (1975--1987), and a member of the Senate Armed

Services Committee. In *The Minuteman: Restoring an Army of the People* (1998), Hart proposes to drastically cut down the size of the professional regular army, by at least two-thirds, to a smaller, rapid-deployment force. The rest would be replaced by citizen reserve forces, "a national militia." *Basic military training would be universal, a part of education, but participation in the military reserves ("militia") would be voluntary.* He believes that a well-trained and equipped reserve system could take over most current military tasks. He understands that this system could not be used for aggressive policies, such as the first Gulf war. Reserve units would be tied to civilian communities and industries For example, he suggests that a proportion of U.S. merchant ships be built so that they could be transformed into navy ships, handled by reserve units of merchant sailors.

The aim of this little history-in-a-nutshell of the concept of an armed nation is to show that the idea has a respectable history, going back to the democratic and socialist traditions, that it has been taken seriously by knowledgeable people for Western Europe and the U.S., and that it has, from time to time, been successfully implemented to defeat regular armies. This does not *prove* it would work, but provides good evidence, I think, for its applicability.

An nonstate society would implement some such program (International Revolutionary Solidarity..., 1980). What kind of military system it had would depend a great deal on the military forms used in the course of the revolution, particularly how much--and what kind-- of a civil war was necessary to defeat the counterrevolution. The armed forces may have had to be more centralized than the libertarians had wanted. The principle is for *an army to be as decentralized and democratic as possible and only as centralized and professional as is necessary.* This is a matter of empirical balance and of conscious political decision-making. The aim is for a military which is internally democratic (including election of officers, at least at the lower levels), directly tied to communities and industrial units, and with a minimal professional cadre. Many specialized units can be composed of people from civilian life. For example, even now, air force pilots often retire to become civilian pilots, while remaining in the air force reserves; there could be a similar relation to codebreakers and computer specialists, etc.

A revolutionary anarchist society would *not* be able to use nuclear bombs or other weapons of mass destruction (chemical or biological warfare). Such methods are immoral, destroying civilians and military alike. They are aimed at the workers and farmers of the opposing country, the very people we would want to appeal to. And they are suicidal. A nuclear attack on our part courts a nuclear response. Just *having* nuclear weapons tempts a first-strike nuclear blow at us by an enemy, for fear of our using them. Even a one-sided use of nuclear weapons would result in radioactive fallout which would spread throughout the world, poisoning those who sent the bombs as well as those bombed.

Paul Nitze, the chief arms control negotiator for the Reagan administration (and therefore no pacifist) declared that the U.S. should "unilaterally get rid of our nuclear weapons" (1999, p. A31). Aside from being dangerous, expensive, and immoral, he argues, they are unnecessary. The accuracy of our conventional weapons is now so great (within three feet, he says) that the U.S. government could destroy any target it chose with nonnuclear means. Therefore the nuclear arsenal is unneeded for either deterrence or attack.

The major defense of a free society would not be in bombs or in military organization but in politics, in its appeal to the populations of other lands. The very fact of dismantling our nuclear weapons would be a powerful political message, as we say to the people of the world, "We are destroying the hell bombs that were built by the capitalist state. We are abandoning our ability to destroy you. We are creating a new society. Do not let your rulers use you to attack us! Disarm them! Overthrow their states! Join us in a free world!" A revolution--especially in the U.S., the center of world imperialism--would have a tremendous political impact throughout the world. Foreign soldiers sent to destroy us would become "infected" by the revolution. Foreign governments would fear to send their forces against a free North America, lest they be destroyed by guerrilla war, defense-in-depth, sabotage, nonviolent resistance, and by revolutionary propaganda. This would be our "deterrence." Our freedom would be our best defense.

* * *

The popular militia would also be part of the anarchist program for controlling "crime," that is, antisocial actions by demoralized people. The militia would take the place of most of the police, at least the patrolling of the streets and keeping the peace. From the evidence of "crime watch" programs (whatever their limitations), *popular participation in crime control, even under current conditions, can be very effective in decreasing antisocial crimes.*

Many people falsely think that the central issue in anarchism is doing away with the police. They think of anarchism as society just as it is but without police--which would result in chaos and violence against working people, until organized crime took over as the new state. Indeed there are pro-capitalist "libertarians" who advocate just such a society, without a state but with everything else the same (Rothbard, 1978). Instead, socialist-anarchists want a totally different society in all areas. But still the problem remains that there will be antisocial, demoralized, and vicious people created by the previous capitalist society who have to be dealt with for some time. Anarchists do not accept revenge or punishment as a social goal, but do accept the need to protect people. Kropotkin's previous statement referred to associations formed for the sake of "mutual protection." How this will be done depends on various local conditions. Communities and regions will try different methods.

When dealing with the question of crime, police, courts, and prisons, the question is not whether it is possible to immediately and completely abolish all coercion--which I doubt--but whether we can dispense with the state. Is it possible to replace the bureaucratic system of "justice," the established courts, lawyers, and the vast body of specialized police, which stand over and against the population of working people... without become victims of aggressive individuals? *Under socialist-anarchism, crime control and policing would be managed by local self-*

Wayne Price

governing communities, with different communities experimenting with various approaches.

"What will be done with those individuals who undoubtedly will persist in violating the social law by invading their neighbors? The anarchists answer that the abolition of the state will leave in existence a defensive association,...on a voluntary basis, which will restrain invaders by any means that may prove necessary." So wrote Benjamin Tucker in 1893 (in Kimmerman & Perry,1966, p. 255).

Without imagining that everyone will become saintly, it can be said that crimes will decrease under anti-authoritarian socialism. Property crimes should certainly go down in a society of plenty, with full employment, at least a minimum guaranteed income, and the social pressures of cooperative small communities. To the extent that communities approximate free-communism, property crimes will vanish, for who will steal when goods can be freely taken off the shelves of the community warehouse?

In a society committed to freedom, many acts currently considered illegal will be legal: the "victimless crimes." We have no right to force people to be good "for their own sake." Moral laws will end, including laws against sexual practices among consenting adults, the prohibition of drugs, and anti-drinking laws such as those against "public intoxication." That covers most of what people currently get arrested for. This does not mean that we stop fighting drug addiction and alcoholism, but these would be seen as public health problems, similar to the spread of AIDS. They would be dealt with by education, public medical measures, and--where necessary--by community regulation. (At present, we cannot regulate the sale of drugs, because of their absolute ban; as a result, it is often easier to buy drugs than alcohol, which *is* regulated.) If addicts could get drugs through controlled medical sources, not only would they not have to steal to maintain their habits, but a whole criminal industry would collapse, as did the Mafia-run smuggling of alcohol after the repeal of Prohibition.

A society without poverty, racism, and sexism would have much less--if any--drug addiction, alcoholism, and nonconsensual sex. Even now, the extent of crime is mostly in response to social conditions, not to policing. For example, in the US, the state with the very lowest crime rate is North Dakota (*New York Times,* September 9, 1996). It has the lowest rate for murder or any other violent crimes, the lowest robbery rate, and the lowest proportion of prisoners: one out of a thousand (the national rate is one out of 167). It had fewer than 100 incidents of violent crime per hundred thousand inhabitants in 1994. By contrast, California had over a thousand incidents per hundred thousand inhabitants. There were eight murders in all of North Dakota in 1995. People are proud of leaving their doors, bikes, and cars unlocked. They have the lowest car insurance in the nation. And crime rates are at essentially the same levels as fifteen years ago. As a result, policing is much less than elsewhere. It wasn't until 1995 that they created the office of state medical examiner to do autopsies. "A member of the North Dakota parole board...sometimes feels a bit like the fabled Maytag repairman" (*New York Times,* September 21, 1996).

The *New York Times* article raises possible reasons for this low crime rate, including the fact that North Dakota is cold--not a reproducible factor. More relevantly, most people live in rural, small communities. A tribal judge for the Spirit Lake Sioux says, "One of the reasons that crime is so low in North Dakota is that people are so close-knit. You get a bank robber or a shady character come into town, and he stands out like a sore thumb." Other things mentioned are the stable, two-parent families, low divorce rate, and supportive, extended families. Finally, it has a very low unemployment rate, less than half the national average. This is not a utopia and many people might not want to live as traditionally as the North Dakotans do--while many might. My point is that *a society with close-knit communities, full employment, and supportive social relations, can create a low-crime, minimal-police situation.* The article summarizes, "North Dakota, in large part, is on the honor system." We can create a whole society which is (in large part) on the honor system.

Anarchist communities will have rules and regulations--"laws"--passed by popular assemblies. These will be enforced by popular participation:

local working people who take turns in the community militia. There may be some specialists, such as school crossing guards assigned by a public school's council or jujitsu experts to train the militia members in self-defense. There may be a forensic laboratory. Some communities may chose to have the equivalent of local sheriffs. Shalom (2004), an advocate of a post-statist polity consistent with "parecon," argues that a citizen army would not be appropriate. There would continue to be some need, he feels, for specially trained, sensitive, and democratically controlled police. Perhaps. But *it would be essential not to create a cadre of special police who feel antagonistic to the general working population.*

Individuals may still commit violent, antisocial acts--although fewer than before. Especially in the period after the revolution, there may be many who have been twisted by the previous capitalist society. The basic principle is that *society has a right to protect itself, but not to punish people.* We may defend ourselves against antisocial individuals, but we should give up ancient concepts of revenge and retaliation. Individual victims may still feel vengeful, naturally, but this is not what a society should base its policies on. (Being against punishment does not mean being against personal responsibility. Antisocial actors, however much they have been victims in the past, need to be led to take responsibility for their acts--only then can they stop being victims.)

Once caught, accused people would be brought before a community court. Perhaps there would be an elected or hired judge. Members of the jury might be the whole assembly or a selected part of one. This would be a criminal case. Civil cases, disputes between individuals within the community, might go before the same type of court, or might use independent arbitrators whom both sides accept (even now a large proportion of business disputes are taken before arbitrators rather than state courts). Judges would be guided by the community's rules and by the precedents of reasonable decisions made by other judges: the "common law."

If an individual is convicted of an antisocial act, the community would attempt to resolve its effects by means of reconciliation between the offender and the victim, restitution by the offender to the victim, or by public confession and repentance. Public service may be assigned, a job offered, and counseling provided. There may be some form of modified probation--living in the community but under supervision. (There are people committed to prison abolition who have thought about alternatives to incarceration and have already experimented with some of them; Morris, 1976; Pepinsky & Quinney, 1991). If individuals show, by their deeds, that society needs to protect itself against them, they may have to be restrained in community group homes or--as a very last resort--residential institutions (small prisons). However, *the vast network of large prisons will be torn down.*

The "rehabilitation" of prisoners is a joke in our society. Prisoners are more likely to commit crimes after being incarcerated than before. Prisons have pretty much given up any goals except keeping a large number of people off the streets, as cheaply as possible. "Rehabilitation" assumes that we have a good, healthy society, and that all will be well if these aberrant individuals, the criminals, adjust themselves to it. Instead we have a sick society, whose antisocial values of getting ahead by getting over are common to car thieves and big businesspeople, and macho violence is glorified in war and the media, a society which creates pools of misery underneath its middle class prosperity, where racism and sexism are rampant and roads to success are closed off for the poor and People of Color. *Of course*, rehabilitation does not work and prisons are schools of crime.

But in a truly free and cooperative society, the rehabilitation of criminals becomes a reasonable goal. Where people are valued, and racism and sexism are fought, and the predominant values are of cooperation, and jobs and a decent living are available to all--anti-social individuals *will* be aberrant. It will be reasonable to ask people to take responsibility for their actions and to join society. This cannot be done by the methods of today's courts and prisons, but a new society will try hard to find suitable methods.

More important than rehabilitation is long-term prevention. As a post-revolutionary freed people work to abolish poverty and oppression, they will also overcome child abuse and neglect. Emotionally cold antisocial people are created by loveless maltreatment of children. A massive social program, run by every community, would protect every child (Kellerman, 1999). Efforts would be made to reintegrate troubled families, if at all possible, with coaching for parents where needed. Warm and caring foster homes are an alternative. However, many abandoned or overwhelming children may do best in residential communal homes, youth houses, or therapeutic group facilities run by responsible adults. Actually, many children--or at least adolescents-- might like to be able to leave their families to go live in a youth house for a while, if they had the option.

A special effort would have to be made to identify dangerous children, young people at risk for violent antisocial behavior (Kellerman, 1999). Communal agencies would pick out youngsters who show precocious aggression or viciousness, as long before adolescence as possible. (Under capitalism, such programs are excuses for racism, but we are postulating a post-capitalist society.) Special therapeutic, educational, and medical programs could prevent their ever developing into the kind of demoralized predators who exist in authoritarian society.

* * *

How will a socialist-anarchist society *coordinate* itself without a state? There will be some degree of economic planning and of regulation of enterprises. This has been sometimes expressed as the "administration of things, not of people" (although it is hard to imagine how things can be "administered" without coordinating people!). At the local level--in the community or the factory--the coordinating body would be the people themselves in their assembly. Higher levels of the federated Commune would be composed of delegates from the assemblies. Their focus would be on the tasks they were elected to deal with, such as economic coordination.

Revolutions have repeatedly given the same answer. Again and again they have thrown up popular councils. These include rank-and-file councils run by face-to-face direct-democracy. Such were the neighborhood assemblies of Paris during the French revolution or the shop-floor factory councils formed in the Russian revolution and then formed again in Germany and Italy. The local, self-governing communities sent delegates to common centers--people who are easily recalled and who are paid workers' wages. These in turn sent delegates to higher level councils. Such workers' councils (or worker, peasant, and soldier councils) were created again during the 1936 Spanish revolution and then the 1956 Hungarian revolution and other revolts in Eastern Europe. Workers' councils developed during the Chilean struggle of the seventies and repeatedly during other South American struggles. The latest are the factory occupations of Argentina and its neighborhood assemblies.

Shalom (2004) proposes a system of "nested councils." Primary councils, in the communities, would include between 25 to 50 people, and all adults in the society would be members. The size is necessary to permit face-to-face discussion and decision-making. Each council sends delegates to second-level councils, also of no more than 50. These councils would send delegates to higher levels, and so on, until the whole nation (at least) is covered. Unlike many anarchists, he does not propose that delegates be bound by mandates telling them how they must vote. That would prevent real deliberations which might change delegates' minds and alter decisions. (Anarchists might propose that higher level councils might have to send decisions down to lower levels to be okayed before being accepted, although this could slow everything down considerably.)

Some sort of council system, rooted in the direct democracy of local communities and shop floor committees, creates a flexible and radically democratic form of social coordination. Popular control over "leaders" may be maintained; there can be frequent turnover of official personnel. Different parties (or political organizations which are not parties) may be represented in proportion to their support among the oppressed sectors of society. Changes in popular political opinions are easily and rapidly reflected in the composition of the delegated councils. Thus it is easy for parties (or nonparties) to peacefully change places--

in particular, for revolutionary organizations, starting as minorities, to expand their influence.

Exactly how a new council system would actually be set up during a revolution will depend on the particular circumstances. Some advocate that councils be mainly based in neighborhoods and communities. Others, in the anarchist-syndicalist tradition, advocate that they be mainly based in factories, offices, and other workplaces. Methods of election and representation may vary from region to region even within one country. This is also a strength of the federal council system.

Anarchists believe in the great importance of local, self-governing, institutions, with direct, face-to-face, democracy, whether on the shop floor or in the community. Elected people will have to be sent to higher levels of the federation, but the federation must be rooted in daily direct democracy--democracy as a "way of life." For almost all of the existence of the human species, we have lived in small communities: in hunter-gathering tribal units or in villages. This is what we evolved for. Most cities, when they began, were in the tens of thousands. Cities of over a million are very recent, created by the Industrial Revolution. As decentralists, anarchists wish to combine the advantages of a modern urban, postindustrial, lifestyle, including freedom of movement, with decentralized direct democracy. This is essential if democracy is to be more than the selection of representatives who will go to distant places to be political *for* us. Instead, democracy, even with elections, must be rooted in the daily decision-making of people.

Thomas Jefferson was impressed by the town meetings of New England. He advocated dividing the counties into smaller "wards," with local control over schools, militia units, policing, maintenance of roads, judge and jury selections, and collecting votes for higher offices. "Where every man [Note] is a sharer in the direction of his ward-republic, or of some of the higher ones, and feels that he is a participator in the government of affairs, not merely at an election one day in the year, but every day; when there shall not be a man in the state who will not be a member of some one of its councils, great or small, he will let the heart be torn out of his body sooner than his power be wrested from him by a Caesar or a Bonaparte" (Jefferson, 1957, p. 54).

How exactly to balance decentralism and centralism in any particular institution is a practical question. We will need both local communes and international associations. In principle, federalism makes both possible, but the proper balance can only be found through social experiment. However the basic principle should be, again, *as much decentralization as possible, and only enough centralization as is absolutely necessary.*

This point was made by Martin Buber in his quirky *Paths in Utopia* (1958). He quoted Lenin, during the Russian revolution: "We must be centralists; yet there will be moments when the task will shift to the provinces; we must leave the maximum of initiative to individual localities...." (in Buber, 1958, p. 109). Buber commented, "Instead of...'We must be centralists, yet there will be moments...,' a genuinely socialist attitude would have put it the other way round: 'We must be decentralists, federalists, autonomists, yet there will be moments when our main task will shift to a central authority because revolutionary action requires it; only we must take care not to let these requirements swamp the objective and temporal frame of reference' " '(Buber, 1958, p. 109). This is exactly right. In contrast to the Marxist view, even during a revolution, we should be only be as centralized as is temporarily necessary.

A decentralized, federalized, democratic system does not require that everyone spend all their time being involved in all decisions, local and federal. Barber (2003) describes an idea of a participatory politics he calls "strong democracy." Its goal is a system where "...all of the people can participate some of the time in some of the responsibilities of governing...."

Needing social coordination does not mean that there has to be a single "sovereign" institution which is supreme over all other institutions because it "represents" all of society. For example, right now there is no world government--internationally we are in a state of "anarchy." The United Nations only functions when the main national governments agree that it should. Yet it is possible to mail letters from anywhere to anywhere on earth. The postal systems of the world's nations have come to a common agreement. Similarly, airplanes fly internationally, business is done internationally, railroad tracks cross all the borders of Europe, telephones communicate internationally, and the Internet functions internationally. Despite rampant nationalism, international conferences have been able to make rules for a wide variety of functions which have tied the world together--without a sovereign world government. (This was a point often made by Kropotkin.)

Even within our capitalist democracy, it is accepted that the state does not have unlimited power over all institutions. For example, given the "wall of separation between church and state," the U.S. state does not endorse, pay for, or intervene in the internal affairs of churches (although they are given tax exemptions). These are major institutions, affecting the lives of millions, which are theoretically parallel to, not under, the state. Similarly, guarantees of civil liberties means that there are major areas of life which are not under the control of the state, except in extreme circumstances. (This is what is accepted in theory; in practice there are many violations of basic rights, of course.)

The guild socialists argued that a free socialism should organize itself industrially in a pluralistic fashion, as opposed to the centralized state socialist model (Cole, 1980; Pateman, 1970; Tawney, 1948). More recently, John Burnheim has advanced a scheme for extreme pluralism which he calls *demarchy*: Decisions currently made by central multifunction agencies from the national to the city level could be made by "autonomous specialized agencies that are coordinated by negotiation among themselves or, if that fails, by quasi-judicial arbitration, rather than by direction from a controlling body." This would include parks, streets, libraries, building regulations, health services, sanitation, run independently. (Burnheim, 1989, pp. 7-8).

In his model, the direction of each agency would be entrusted to those who were directly affected by it (workers and consumers), not the whole community. Nor would the directing committees be elected; they would be chosen by lot from the affected part of the community (sortition). Choosing by lot is how we select juries to this day, and it is how the democracy of ancient Athens selected almost all its officials and committees. This would create a "statistically representative democracy" in which different points of view would be represented according to their spread in the population. Instead of specialized politicians, ordinary people would have the opportunity to directly manage the institutions which dominate their lives.

Again this is something which different regions and nations could experiment with. Some regions would prefer to try a more tightly federated system, with popular organizations merged into a single organization with an overall council. Others may prefer to try a looser network, with organizations parallel to each other, coordinated only by occasional negotiations . Burnheim's idea of selecting officials by lot rather than election does not have to go together with his extreme pluralism. Barber (2003) also advocates that it be tried in various institutions as an alternative to elected representation.

* * *

Anarchism is often criticized for assuming that it is possible for everyone to be good, all the time. This is assumed to be too idealistic, to deny the supposedly sordid reality of human nature. It is true that anarchism does believe that people can adjust to a cooperative and self-managed society. But anarchism does not assume that people can be perfect. On the contrary, anarchism has always held that people cannot be trusted to have power over other people. Speaking against slavery, Abraham Lincoln said, "No man [Note] is good enough to govern another man without that other's consent". Anarchists believe that no one is good enough to govern others even with their consent. "Power corrupts," is a fundamental anarchist belief. Therefore anarchists advocate decentralization, pluralism, free speech and a free press (freedom of all media), direct democracy, only a minimum of representation, and every sort of check and balance to prevent the accumulation of power in the hands of anyone (Goodman, 1965).

It is sometimes asked, what about the *rogue community*? Suppose there is an anarchist federation but some township, commune, or urban enclave opts out, as is its right. What if it then declares itself open only to white people, or it teaches creationism in its schools, or it dumps pollution into the river on which other communities are located? Doesn't this prove that a state is needed to force the community to follow the common good? What would a non-statist society do?

I accept the assumption for the sake of argument, since I have agreed that people will not be perfect under libertarian socialism--although I do expect people to become better than they are now. In this case, I imagine that the other regional communities would have a conference (after local discussions had taken place). Someone would propose that the rogue community be left alone. Let them stew in their own juice. People of Color will have plenty of other places to go to. Its schools will not be accredited by institutions of higher learning if they do not teach evolution. Their pollution can be cleaned up by others, which is better than the alternative of coercion. Some one else, from another town, may declare instead that what that community was doing was intolerable, harming not merely its own interests but that of others. Therefore this person proposes that the regional militia be mobilized from every community and march on the offending community, forcing it to change its policies. Others will say that this is too extreme, there are intermediate possibilities. A propaganda campaign could be organized by the region, to persuade that community's members to change their policies. Nonviolent demonstrations could be held inside the community, causing disruption without violence. An economic boycott of the community could coerce it but without using arms. Depending on the specific circumstances, the regional federation would pick one of the alternative policies.

Marxists and many others imagine that anarchists think they can leap immediately into a completely free, peaceful, and cooperative society (Marx's "higher stage of communism"). This is a caricature of anarchism. As we have seen, anarchists are usually aware of the need for (in Kropotkin's words) "defense of the territory" through an armed population, for "mutual protection" against antisocial persons, and for overall social coordination through an association of councils.

Chapter 6. Technological Challenges to Abolition of the State

Can the abolition of the state be achieved in our age of mass industry? Aside from a generalized distrust of ordinary people's ability to manage themselves, the main argument for the state may be that industrial technology supposedly requires a centralized social order. This view is common to conservatives, liberals, and Marxists. In an introduction to a collection of anarchist writings, Irving Louis Horowitz wrote dismissively, "It scarcely requires any feats of mind to show that *modern industrial life is incompatible with the anarchist demand for the liquidation of state authority*" (1964, p. 26; my emphasis).

A related assertion was made in 1922 by Nikolai Bukharin, then the leading theorist of the Russian Communists after Lenin. In *Anarchy and Scientific Communism,* he wrote that the difference between anarchism and Marxist ("scientific") Communism was *not* over "the final objective" of abolishing the state. Unlike liberals and reform socialists (such as Horowitz), Bukharin believed, "In the [communist] future there will be no classes, there will be no class oppression, and thus no instrument of that oppression, no state..." (Bukharin, 1981, p. 2). The real difference, Bukharin declared, was over (1) the need for a transitional state--the "dictatorship of the proletariat", and (2) how to expand social production in order to produce plenty for all.

"Our ideal solution to this is centralized production, methodically organized in large units and, in the final analysis, the organization of the world economy as a whole. Anarchists, on the other hand, prefer...tiny communes...[and] small, decentralized production which cannot raise, but only lower, the level of these productive forces" (Bukharin, 1981, p. 2 & 4). This amounts to advocating a centralized, bureaucratic, state-like structure indefinitely--on a worldwide scale.

A response to Bukharin's essay was written by the Italian anarchist Luigi Fabbri (1981). He made a number of incisive remarks, including the prediction that the Russian Communist dictatorship, far from withering away, would produce a "state capitalist" system run by a "new ruling class"--this in 1922! He criticized the Marxists' worship of capitalist centralization. A great deal of that is created by the drive for profits, not because centralization is always the most effective form of production. Capitalists centralize for purposes of speculation, for control over the workers, for monopoly over raw materials and over markets, to improve international competitive positions, and for other imperialist and monopolist reasons. (This is even more true in our age of globalization, much of which is technologically unnecessary.)

However, Fabbri denied that anarchists were inflexible about decentralized production. Anarchists wanted production which would fit in with federations of cooperative communities and worker-controlled industries. Therefore they advocated as much decentralized industry as possible. But if some centralization was necessary in some industries, then it was necessary. The anarchist vision "...was reflected also in the organization of production, giving preference *as far as possible* to a decentralized form of organization; but this does not take the form of an absolute rule to be provided everywhere in every instance. A libertarian order would in itself...rule out the possibility of imposing such a unilateral solution" (Fabbri, 1981, p. 23; my emphasis). This statement, regarding technology, is similar to Buber's statement, quoted above, in regard to politics. It is an important principle of the anarchist method.

Marxists claim that there are liberatory possibilities in modern industrial technology, organized in centralized production. For the first time in human history, they say (correctly), technology makes it possible to end all scarcity, hunger, and toil. It has become possible to create a world of plenty for all, with abundant leisure--which, as mentioned, permits the participation of everyone in decision-making. The openly pro-capitalist political tendencies (conservatives and liberals) point out that capitalism produced all this productive technology and therefore, they say, should be kept going. These days even social democrats, while advocating some reforms, do not want to kill the bourgeois goose while it is supposedly laying golden eggs. Marxists point out the continuing poverty and misery around the world, and the economic insecurity even in the industrialized imperialist countries. Only a few get those golden eggs. Technology will only be used for human welfare, they say, when it ceases being "capital" (property owned by a few) and becomes social means of production held in common by the working people. Capitalism must be replaced with a new society--*but* one which will still carry on capitalism's forms of production (under new management, so to speak).

Unfortunately for these celebrations of industrialism, modern technology has more problems than its being monopolized by a few (Commoner, 1972). The golden eggs are also radioactive--and who can eat gold anyway? To repeat: modern technology pollutes the air we breathe and the food we eat; is warming the entire earth, and preparing both droughts and floods; is exterminating whole species of plants and animals and destroying the rain forests; produces waste products, such as plastics and radioactive material, which will last indefinitely; uses up nonrenewable resources; and has produced weapons of such vast destructive power that a war might eliminate all life on earth.

Consider how much of our industrial life is based on petroleum, natural gas, coal, and their byproducts. Our transportation system of cars and trucks and planes runs on gasoline. Our food is produced with massive use of petrochemical fertilizers and pesticides. Our clothes are made, in large part, from synthetic fibers, petroleum-derived. Our homes are heated by natural gas and petroleum. Electricity is made from coal and petroleum. And everywhere, from clothes to furniture, to housing, to all sorts of objects, we use plastic, made from these sources.

Yet petroleum, natural gas, and coal are limited, nonrenewable, resources, bound to run out some day. The world supply of oil is probably going to decline within a decade, or at most two. Their use is polluting the air, causing the greenhouse effect which will flood coastal cities and spread drought to farmlands. Plastics are nonbiodegradable; plastic garbage is likely to last a long, long time. Inevitable oil spills from pipelines and tankers destroy local ecologies. Yet we have permitted these resources to become the basis of our way of life!

There are also evils of current technology which are rarely mentioned even by ecologically-minded critics. One is its effects on workers in the modern factory--not just the on-the-job pollution or the high rate of inevitable accidents, but the very relationship of workers to the machines. Rather than bringing out the creative powers of the individual worker, typical factory machinery is *designed* to make work as mindless and repetitive as possible. The workers are subordinated to the machinery and their work may be defined as whatever would cost too much to do by machine--yet. Other difficulties with current technology relate to the quality of the goods we consume, the layout of our oversized cities, and the overall nature of our "high standard of living."

It will not be enough to pass some laws against pollution. *The entire technological basis of our industrial society--how we physically produce and distribute goods and services--must be transformed.* The problem with modern industrial technology is not only that it is owned by a few, nor even that these few, the capitalists, are driven by the system to produce for monetary profits, to accumulate and grow regardless of their effects on the workers or the environment. These *are* problems, inherent in capitalism. *Social ownership and production for use, not profit, are necessary but not enough.* Marxists say that the capitalist state cannot be simply seized and used to create socialism, but must be replaced by another structure. And they recognize that the capitalist economic system must be overthrown and replaced. But oddly enough, most of them believe that the existing technology can be used as it is, without a basic transformation.

*   *   *

In contrast, there are anarchists and other radicals who have concluded that the whole machinery of industrial technology must be dispensed with. Electricity, automobiles, gas furnaces, power production, airplanes, televisions, computers, and even modern medicine must be abolished. Humanity must return to a level of technology from before the industrial revolution, at least to the technical level of the middle ages or perhaps even to before the agricultural revolution, to hunter-gatherer societies. These technophobes, or "primitivists," share the basic thesis of the Marxists and conventional technophiles: they agree that modern technology can only be centralized (massive, unecological, alienating, and heirarchially-organized). The Marxists and others argue *for* centralization because scientific technology requires it (they think). The technophobes argue *against* scientific technology because it requires centralization (they think).

There is a third viewpoint, which rejects the belief that a scientific, modern, industrialized technology must be centralized and authoritarian. Going back to Kropotkin, it includes Lewis Mumford (1970, 1986), Paul Goodman (1965, 1990), E. F. Schumacher (1999), and Murray Bookchin (1986). They, and others, are as critical of the current use of technology as the "primitivists." They agree that industrial civilization has reached a dead end, morally, ecologically, and humanely, and it threatens the destruction of humanity. But they believe that a scientific technology could be used to create a truly human society. For this, technology must be used in a different style.

The alternate technologists base their view on several premises. One is that modern technology is not only potentially very *productive* (they agree with the Marxist point) but it is potentially very *flexible*. There are different sources of energy (coal and gasoline, but also alcohol, wind, wood, sunlight, tides, and geothermal heating) which can be used to power a few centralized large engines or many decentralized small engines, to spread electrical power on wires over a wide territory, and/or to provide heat and light to large or small communities. Not to mention the demonstration by Lovins (1977) that proper conservation at home and in industry could save a great deal of energy currently wasted. Large factories use enormous machines, but small power tools also exist in many forms and could be used for community workshops (actually the average U.S. factory employed between 40 to 60 workers; of the U.S.'s 275 thousand manufacturing companies, only about 10 percent had 100 or more employees [Morris, 1982]). Transportation today is mostly by car, truck, gasoline-powered ship, and plane, and some railroads, but the railroads could be expanded, trolleys recreated, electric cars built, safe dirigibles and large sailing boats can be built with modern technology. Things that used to be made only of steel can now be made of aluminum or plastic or specially treated woods. Gigantic mainframe computers exist, as do small PCs and even tinier types of computers. The Internet permits imperialist corporations to control operations around the globe, but it also permits bottom-up cooperation from widespread individual PC users. Food can be grown by gigantic factories-in-the-field or by smaller organic farms or by little greenhouses in the middle of cities. Newspapers can be printed in huge printing plants for a few newspaper chains or by desktop publishing for small presses.

Over 40 years ago, Paul and Percival Goodman wrote in *Communitas*, "...For the first time in history we have...a surplus technology, a technology of free choice....We could centralize or decentralize, concentrate population or scatter it....If we want to combine town and country values in an agroindustrial way of life, we can do that.... We could go back to old-fashioned domestic industry with perhaps even a gain in efficiency, for small power is everywhere available, small machines are cheap and ingenious, and there are easy means to collect machined parts and assemble them...." (Goodman and Goodman, 1990, pp. 11--13).

The Goodmans wrote before the growth of the new technology movement. E.F. Schumacher (1999), a key figure, began by investigating projects for economic development. He found that developmental aid went to a few rich locals and government officials, who used it to build massive projects: big dams, factories, and airports. Even when these "worked," they drastically disrupted the local cultures (laying the basis for future fundamentalist religious-nationalist movements). Because these big projects used "advanced" capital-intensive technology, they employed a limited number of people for the money invested. And they were ecologically destructive.

Instead, Schumacher proposed to develop a technology which would help people to develop at their own pace. It would be adapted to countries where capital is scarce but labor is plentiful. It must be inbetween the traditional techniques and the current mass-production methods, what he called an "intermediate technology." In places where farmers used wooden plows pulled by oxen, Schumacher and his colleagues did not offer tractors; instead they developed better steel plows and harness gear for the oxen. They worked on solar-powered metal ovens for farms and villages, and better ways to make small houses using local materials. The idea was to use the best of scientific engineering to develop small machines, small engines, and useful devices which satisfied local needs and relied on local labor and materials to put to use. A whole intermediate technology industry has grown throughout the world.

Under the slogan, "Small is Beautiful," Schumacher and his co-thinkers began to apply his approach to the rich counties also. Now it was called "appropriate technology" or "alternate technology" (or "community" or "soft" or "liberatory technology"). They showed, *by demonstration,* that modern technological principles could be used to make machinery which was decentralized, ecological, conservative of natural resources, and lent itself to worker-control (Davis, 1978; Sale, 1980, 1985). They demonstrated, in the title of one book, that *Small is Possible* (McRobie, 1981).

Similarly, Karl Hess and his friends demonstrated the possibility of decentralized, community-oriented, technology, in a poor neighborhood of Washington, D.C. (Hess, 1979). They built hydroponics, greenhouse gardens on rooftops to grow vegetables and aquariums in a basement to grow fish for meat. They built small, self-contained, bacteriological toilets as an alternate to the conventional sewer system and a basis for turning local human waste into useful fertilizer. They built a solar collector out of catfood cans. This was done in conjuncture with building a community organization, run by direct democracy, where the people who voted on projects were the ones who carried them out. Their work was continued by the Institute for Local Self-Reliance. This advocated turning cities and neighborhoods into industrially self-reliant communities through alternate technology and local economic planning (Morris, 1982).

Theorists of alternate technology have varying politics. Some are plainly pro-capitalist, such as Lovins (1977). Others, such as Hess (1979) or Sale (1980), are apparently neutral between capitalism and a cooperative, production-for-use. economy. Bookchin (1980) is explicitly for a socialist (or small-c communist) anarchism. Goodman (1965) called himself a "community anarchist" and advocated a "mixed economy." Schumacher's politics were sort of decentralist social-democratic; he was influenced by R.H. Tawney, a guild socialist (Tawney, 1948; Cole, 1980). While accurately criticizing the Marxists for their one-sided emphasis on politics and economics, Schumacher and similar technological specialists have tended to argue as if a change in technology, and the size of institutions, were *the* most important areas of change. Instead, small-scale, alternate technology is only one part of an integrated program of revolutionary change--although an essential part (Dickson, 1974). The Small-Is-Beautiful, alternate technology movement has done a lot to demonstrate, in theory and practice, that a decentralized, humanistic technology is practical and *could be chosen.*

The alternate-technologists reject the idea that centralized production is always the most efficient--a capitalist myth which the Marxists have bought completely. It is false if "efficiency" does not mean "most profitable" or "most useful for political control by a few." The meaning of "efficiency" I use means productive of useful

87

goods and services, productive of creative and fulfilling lives by the workers, capable of being democratically controlled, and productive of a balanced ecology.

In particular, increasing concentration of production may indeed make production cheaper, due to "economies of scale," as has been argued. But, *as the costs of production go down, the costs of transportation and distribution increase.* ("Borsodi's Law," Goodman & Goodman, 1990).

So, a gigantic widget factory, using large supplies of widget-material, with gigantic machines and many workers, can make many widgets cheaply. But first it had to assemble the raw materials from sources scattered around the country or the world and bring them to the central factory. These materials have to be stored and transported on the way. Since there are too many workers to live close to the factory, they have to commute twice daily from great distances. Once produced, those widgets have to be shipped around the world to consumers. They must be packaged, containerized, stored in warehouses at various places along their journey, and transported by trains, trucks, ships, and planes. All this commuting, packing, storing, and transporting in two directions uses up resources.

By contrast (going to the other extreme in imagination), consider many small, widely-scattered, widget-making workshops using small power tools and small engines. They could use local supplies of raw materials, as well as recycle local used-up widgets or other waste which uses similar materials. The small number of workers could live nearby, and therefore do not have to travel as far. As a small, local plant or workshop, its widgets would be locally consumed, also cutting down on packing, transportation, and storing. As production is for local use, the shop could expand or cut back on production depending on the short-term demand, which also cuts down on storage needs. To find out whether any particular product ("widget") is really cheaper to make locally or centrally requires a concrete calculation of the expenses of production versus those of distribution--instead of the usual assumption that mass production is automatically cheaper.

This argument was raised by the decentralist Ralph Borsodi (1972) during the 'twenties and 'thirties. The Borsodi family went to live on a homestead, a mostly self-sufficient farm. They did this originally for cultural and political purposes, to create an alternative to our "ugly civilization." To their surprise, they discovered that much of their work, using the then-latest power tools, was more efficient than mass production! Thus Borsodi calculated that canned tomatoes, grown and canned by his wife, were cheaper than store-bought canned tomatoes (counting her hours of labor at standard wages). He started calculating the costs of other items they used for food, clothing, and shelter. By his estimates, a third of the national product was more effectively made centrally, by mass production, but two-thirds of was cheaper to make on homesteads, Given his homesteading political program, he did not calculate how much might be cheaper to make at intermediary community or regional levels, which was probably a great deal. Of course, capitalist economists do not make such calculations today, although the appropriate-technologists have shown that a large part of modern industrial products could be effectively produced locally or regionally. It is probably much more than Borsodi's two-thirds evaluation.

When discussing the supposed efficiency of centralized mass production, centralists usually do not include its distorting effects on the ecology, including its poisonous wastes and its consumption of nonrenewable resources. When calculating costs of production, they do not include the expenses that will have to be made eventually to clean up the environment. Pollution is counted as an "externality," that is, it is the community, not the capitalist firm, which is expected to pay to clean it up. In general, a single large factory--going back to the example of widget production--produces a lot of the same kind of waste, concentrated in one spot. This is more difficult to absorb than the same amount of waste produced in small amounts in many different places by smaller plants. Further, a planned, local economy can make an effort to examine community waste products and see how they can be recycled for productive purposes (Morris, 1982). Plastics, precisely because of the durability which makes them so difficult to get rid of, can be recycled by local manufacturing into new products. Human and animal wastes, as well as organic garbage, can be recycled into fertilizer for local farms and gardens.

* * *

Questions of efficiency in industrial production include the human organization of the process of production. Integrally related to the machinery are the human beings who work them (or who are worked by them). Industry is centralized and hierarchical, with the workers serving on the bottom of a chain of command. There they carry out orders, doing assigned jobs, given as little room for initiative as possible, doing jobs on or off the assembly line which are broken down into minute tasks.

Yet capitalists are so driven to improve profits that they have even tried giving workers more democratic control over production. The capitalists have hired industrial psychologists or sociologists to experiment with the human production process. Tasks are added together to make them more interesting (job enrichment), or the workers can take turns doing different jobs (job rotation), or they are given more say over how the work is done, individually or in small groups (job enlargement). Over the decades, such experiments have consistently shown improvements in production, rises in worker morale, decreases in turnover and absenteeism, and improvement in job satisfaction. Such experiments have been done with workers in assembly-line factories, office workers, scientists, and salespeople (Jenkins, 1974). They have been done with employees at a wide range of education. The most extreme "experiments" have been studies of group contracts in Europe or the US, that is, where workers are hired as a group to do a job and they organize themselves to use the machines and then divide the pay among themselves.

"The link between greater participation of workers...and greater productivity rises to the level of a truism....An extensive review of the literature...found consistent support for the view that worker participation in management causes higher productivity'" (Grenier, 1988, p. 127).

The logic of such social experiments is to advocate *worker democracy*, which is why these experiments are never allowed to lead to anything under capitalism. They provide the evidence that workers could control industry on a day-to-day, shopfloor, level. If so, then why do we need capitalists, bureaucrats, or the state?

Which answers the question, if decentralization and democratization are so efficient, why don't the capitalists do it? Another answer is that sometimes they do. As just mentioned, the capitalists have repeatedly tried democratization of production. And big corporations often decide to break up the management of their operations into separate, smaller, groupings. Most giant corporations chose to handle much of their operations through small contractors rather than doing everything themselves. Decentralist technology is often developed by conventional businesses (consider the growth of home computers through the usual market forces).

But all these forces have their limits. Capitalist firms must dominate their workers or they would not be capitalist. Competition drives them to try to dominate their markets. They must grow or be gobbled up by the firms which do grow. That is, there are reasons of finance and power which require centralization, hierarchy, and gigantism.   Therefore, capitalist firms look for technology which serves centralization, hierarchy, and gigantism. If a stateless society chooses to, it can look for technology which serves decentralization, democracy, and smallness. The problem is not the technology but the type of society.

After a revolution, the workers should begin immediately to reorganize and rebuild technical production (Castoriadis,1988). Otherwise class relations would be recreated. Advocates of "parecon" propose creating "balanced job complexes" where jobs would be reconfigured to include mental and manual labor, aiming to make job satisfaction as equal as possible for everyone (Albert, 2003). Starting from what we have, workers and others will recreate the production process to be easier for workers to manage, to do away with the division between mental and manual labor, to make work creative and interesting for the workers, to make products which are socially useful, to make production ecologically safe and healthful.

In a passage which has been almost universally ignored by Marxists, Engels wrote: "...Society cannot free itself unless every individual is freed. The old mode of production must therefore be revolutionized from top to bottom, and in particular the former division of labor must disappear. Its place must be taken by an organization of production... which... instead of being a means of subjugating men [Note], will become a means of their emancipation, by offering each individual the opportunity to develop all his facilities, physical and mental, in all directions and exercise them to the full--in which, therefore, productive labor will become a pleasure instead of being a burden" (Engels, 1954, p. 408).

This is what the revolution is for.

Chapter 7: The Experimental Society

Marx's concept of the transitional state (or semi-state) is tied up with his concept of the transitional economy. "We are dealing here with a communist society, not as it has developed on its own foundations, but on the contrary, just as it emerges from capitalist society. In every respect, economically, morally, intellectually, it is thus still stamped with the birthmarks of the old society from whose womb it has emerged" (*Critique of the Gotha Program*, in Marx 1974, p. 346). Quite an image! but we get his point.

Coming out of capitalism, he believed, it is not possible to immediately create "a more advanced phase of communist society" (same, p. 347). It will be necessary for a while, in "the first phase of communist society"(same), to have a system in which workers are still paid according to the amount of work they do, until productivity reaches a higher level. Aspects of the market, driven by the law of value, will continue, gradually being displaced by conscious planning of the economy. A "dictatorship of the proletariat" will be needed during this transitional period--usually interpreted as a new state. (It was Lenin, and not Marx, who labeled Marx's "first phase of communist society" as "socialism" and only the "more advanced phase" as "communism." Leftists today have usually accepted Lenin's terms. I use "socialism" as a broader term which includes "communism.") However, many anarchists, beginning with Kropotkin, have argued that it is possible to go immediately into a fully communist economy, that a semi-communist transitional system--half capitalist and half socialist, so to speak--would not work (because it is impossible to decide how much the labor of each worker is worth in modern collective production) and is unnecessary (because full communism could be immediately implemented).

Bakunin appears to have believed in a transitional stage before an ultimate goal of anarchist communism. After Bakunin's death, his friend James Guillame summarized Bakunin's views of a post-revolutionary society. The goal of libertarian communism, he believed, would depend on achieving a high enough level of productivity. "In the meantime, each community will decide for itself during the transition period the method they deem best for the distribution of the products of associated labor" (in Bakunin, 1980, p. 362).

It is many years since Marx or Bakunin. Since then, capitalism has developed technology to the point of extremely high productivity, surely enough for a libertarian communist society. This is especially true if socialism (communism) got rid of all the waste produced under capitalism. Instead of so many varieties of automobiles, there could be a few alternate varieties plus an expanded train, bus, and trolley system (and an effort to get people to live closer to work in communities which integrate work and life). International socialism would get rid of the trillions of dollars wasted regularly on armament production. And there are a vast number of jobs which would no longer be necessary: all the tribes of middle and upper management, the insurance industry, the advertising business, etc. Vast numbers of people would be free to work at productive labor, producing more while lightening the burden on all.

The post-revolutionary society would begin with a technology of immense productivity, an end to capitalist waste, and an expanded productive work force. It can be argued that it would be possible to immediately implement libertarian communism without waiting for the further development of technology. Potentially modern technology is so productive that it could provide everyone with a high standard of living while requiring a very small amount of the total social labor.

(Something similar to our agricultural productivity, by which 1 % of the population now produces far more than enough for all of North America, even though, for most of human history, it took 99 % of the population to do this).

What then? No one would *need* to labor due to lack of food, clothing, etc. But people would not be content to be idle while robots do all the work. People will want to be active. There will be far more volunteers than there will be "necessary" jobs! There will be a need to "create" occupations, to combine work and play into creative crafts. Activities (I would not call them simply "labor") will be done to develop human potentialities (as in *News from Nowhere* by William Morris, 1986).

Potentially this is true. Unfortunately this highly productive technology is not immediately available everywhere. Most of the world is not really industrialized. A post-revolutionary society would have to help the once oppressed nations to develop--in an ecologically sustainable fashion, according to the needs of the local people. Even in the industrialized nations (the former imperialist countries), there will be a need to transform existing technology in an ecological, self-manageable, fashion. Plus, revolutions may turn into destructive civil wars if there is much resistance. *Much rebuilding may be necessary once the revolution is won.* Also, if it takes time for the revolution to spread from its first countries to the rest of the world, there will be capitalist states side-by-side with free societies; therefore arms production will still be needed. All this may limit how quickly the workers can create a society so immensely productive that there would be no need for placing limits on most consumption.

Until productivity is universally high enough, there will be the question of motivating workers to do the labor necessary for the survival of society. As much as possible, workers will change necessary labor into creative and interesting activity. The revolution will develop idealistic motivations. It is easier to see the value of one's work when living in relatively smaller communities--which will have to be built. Yet popular psychology will not change overnight, and, it has been argued, there may be a need for rewarding effort in order to keep people working.

* * *

The reported view of Bakunin leads into a third position, besides a transitional system or an immediate leap into full communism: that of an *experimental economy.* The capitalists will be expropriated and the economy will be some form of cooperative, collectivized, form, democratically managed by those who work in it. But exactly how this will work out may not be the same at every time and place.

The anarchist-communist Errico Malatesta noted that we could not assume that everyone, or even most workers, would be persuaded of libertarian communism even after a revolution. The revolution will probably be made as a united front. To try to *impose* libertarian communism on everyone would be an atrocity, a mockery of the very idea. Instead many approaches may be tried (so long as exploitation is not accepted), until the people settle on the best, out of their own experience.

Malatesta wrote, "Probably every possible form of possession and utilization of the means of production and all ways of distribution of produce will be tried out at the same time in one or many regions, and they will combine and be modified in various ways until experience will indicate which form, or forms, is or are the most suitable....So long as one prevents the...consolidation of new privilege, there will be time to find the best solutions..." (1984, p. 104).

He also wrote, "...One must consider *anarchy above all as a method*....Only anarchy points the way along which they can find, by trial and error, that solution which best satisfies...the needs and wishes of everybody.... How will children be educated? We don't know. So what will happen? Parents, pedagogues, and all who are concerned... will come together, will discuss, will agree or divide according to the views they hold, and will put into practice the methods which they think are the best. And with practice that method which in fact is the best, will in the end be adopted. And similarly with all problems which present themselves" (Malatesta, 1974, pp. 45 & 47; my emphasis).

It is unlikely that there is one best way which fits each and every industry, the production of steel as well as the education of children. It is unlikely that there is one best way which fits every culture and region on earth, regardless of national history or traditions or climate or available natural resources. A major advantage of a federalized, pluralistic, system is that different localities can try out different approaches to common issues. Different regions can learn from each others' successes and failures. Such a society could be considered "transitional," only in the sense that it is always in transition, always changing.

Many different social forms can be tried out, so long as they stay within certain broad limits, that of remaining truly democratic, decentralized, cooperative, and non-exploitative--that is, that society remains free to continue to experiment. Referring back to previous statements by Buber and Fabbri, the principle should be *to be as decentralized and democratic and cooperative as possible, to be only as centralized and hierarchical as minimally necessary.* As Paul Goodman put it, "We might adopt a political maxim: to decentralize where, how, and how much [as] is expedient. But where, how, and how much are empirical questions. They require research and experiment" (1965, p. 27). (Much of my thinking on this was first inspired by Goodman. However, as a reformist, he is thinking in terms of experimental, gradual, changes in *this* society, rather than after a workers' revolution--which I, like Malatesta, Bakunin, and Marx, believe necessary.)

Different communities, regions, or nations might try out various models of anti-authoritarian socialism, adapted to their conditions. One such model, as has been mentioned, is the free-communist economy. Everyone works, not for money but because they like to keep active and productive, or because they feel responsible, or because they do not want to be called "lazy bums"--and if a very few do no work, so what? People might take turns doing the dirtiest jobs. Consumption of plentiful goods is free; people take what they want from the shelves. Nobody takes more than they need, since they can always get more.

Scarce goods have to be rationed. To work, such a society needs to produce goods at a high quantity compared to the accepted standard of living; too much rationing and it would falter. A working example is the Israeli kibbutzim, which have lasted for decades.

Alternately, a socialist community might pay workers in credits for hours worked, with pay being adjusted to maintain incentives for various jobs. This is done in B.F. Skinner's *Walden Two* (1962), which suggests how a small socialist community might work (although his model lacks any democracy).

For anything even close to the libertarian communist model, there would be the question of how to coordinate the production and consumption of goods. There could be more or less central planning by elected or appointed officials, with more or less democratic input. Too much central planning runs into the danger of bureaucracy, inflexibility, and authoritarianism. Too little raises the danger of a revival of the market. It should be possible to combine economic planning with decentralized democracy. The early Tennessee Valley Authority is an example. Castoriadis (1997) proposed the use of a central planning mechanism, a "plan factory," which would develop one or more economic plans, to then be debated and decided on by the federation of workers' councils.

Albert and Hahnel (1991; Albert, 2003) have proposed a system of "decentralized socialist planning" or "participatory economics" ("Parecon"). Local consumer councils would list their wants. So would factory councils, listing what materials they need for production. The factory councils would state what they could produce. Using computers and Internet communication, the consumers' wants and the producers' abilities would be balanced, through several cycles of mutual adjustment, as they take each others' projections into consideration. This would be helped by the fact that the consumers and producers are ultimately the same people. Eventually a plan would be developed, without any central planning bureaucracy (although there would be "facilitation boards" which would help the process along). This would avoid the evils of either bureaucratic state planning or of so-called market socialism. It would not be a (small-c) communist society because people would be rewarded according to amount of work they did--excepting children, the disabled, retirees, etc.

The payment (or "remuneration") approach of "Parecon" sounds similar to that proposed by Marx for the lower stage of communism. Unlike the Parecon-ists, however, Marx was clear that this still continued basic bourgeois norms (without a bourgeoisie), as "equal" amounts of labor were exchanged for equal units of goods. He regarded this as only a temporary period until full communism was reached--unlike Albert and Hahnel.

We could imagine a society which "pays" people for their work, while gradually *increasing the free-communist sector of their economy.* Even under capitalism, most roads, public schools, libraries, fire protection, and public water are "free"--that is, communally paid for and available to all. A socialist society might expand this "free" sector, providing basic food, clothing, and shelter for all regardless of work. It has been proposed by Goodman that such a free-communist system (a version of a "guaranteed annual income") should exist side-by-side with a market or other economy (Goodman & Goodman, 1990). Everyone would work in the guaranteed-subsistence sector for, say, a year, to receive lifetime protection. With automation, probably no one would really *have* to work in the substance sector; it could be run either by volunteers or by people paid very little extra. Similarly Fotopoulos (1997) proposes that there be a "basic needs sector" which performs on "the communist principle," while there is is also a "non-basic needs sector" which functions as an artificial "market" which balances supply and demand. Each worker would earn personalized basic-need vouchers and personalized non-basic-need vouchers, the former for doing a minimum of work in basic-needs industry, and the latter for however much work the person does. While either dual system might be considered, I am suggesting, instead, that, as productivity increases, this communist/ basic-needs sector may expand until it covers almost all goods and services: the higher phase of communism.

The smaller the area being planned for, the easier it should be to include popular participation. A local community--a kibbutz or socialist township--could arrange its production and consumption fairly easily, and decide on a plan at the town meeting. Planning for a bioregion, or for a country the size of the U.S., would be much more difficult and it would be harder to avoid bureaucratic tendencies. So it is advisable to keep a planned economy as decentralized as possible. (Albert and Hahnel reject a need for decentralization of community planning or technology. This is also a flaw in their Parecon program, I believe.)

An alternate model might be called "decentralized market socialism." There would be a market, regulated by communal authorities, but big corporations or state enterprises would not be allowed. There is to be no exploitation; workers do not sell their labor power to bosses. Instead, the economy would consist of worker-run businesses (producer cooperatives), consumer cooperatives, small businesses with individual owners, craft shops, community-owned enterprises, and family farms. Something like this has been advocated by some Greens (Spretnak & Capra, 1986) and by Dahl (1985). The concept of a "market socialism" has been advocated for some time, as a practical way of organizing a state-run economy (Lange & Taylor, 1964; Nove, 1983). Its advocates were not thinking of a system of producer cooperatives, but of a centrally planned economy which deliberately imitated a market. Yet most of their argument is applicable here. Using the market would keep the need for central planning to a minimum of regulation. The argument against this approach is that it would discourage solidarity, encourage selfishness, increase inequality, and finally reproduce capitalism.

State-Communist Yugoslavia had such a system, with factories being socially owned but run by worker councils, which hired professional managers. Wage schedules and profit-sharing were worked out within each enterprise. Enterprises competed on the national market, with overall regulation by the state (which was a dictatorship). This had the weaknesses of a market economy, including business cycles, unemployment, inequality between more successful and less successful enterprises, and inequality between regions (which fueled the eventual rise of rabid nationalisms after Tito's death). However, the system worked for many decades, at least as well as the traditional capitalist countries and better than the Communist state-run economies. (I do not know what happened to this system after the collapse of Titoism and the following civil wars.)

I am extremely skeptical about such a system. The economy is not really democratically managed. Instead it is run by the ultimately uncontrollable market. I am just listing this as a possibility for experiment by those regions which wish to try it.

As mentioned, there is hardly a type of industry or enterprise which has not been successfully managed by producers' and/or consumers' cooperatives, working within the market economy. One example is the large and highly successful Mondragon coop in the Basque region of Spain, established in 1956 (Johnson & Whyte, 1982; Morrison, 1995). It includes several productive enterprises, retail coops, a credit union, and a technical college. Other examples can be found in the literature about producer and consumer cooperatives (for example, Lindenfeld & Rothschild-Whitt, 1982). To repeat, cooperatives have worked so well that they tend to become fully integrated into the capitalist system. They have also worked well in all sorts of enterprises in oppressed countries (Maslennikov, 1983).

I am neither advocating or opposing any of these models . I have preferences, for anything which moves toward anarchist-communism, but I do not *know* which is best. Under the right circumstances, any of them may work. Following a revolution, I hope that different regions would try particular models, becoming social experiments from which the world can learn. I am proposing that, *instead of seeing a post-revolutionary society as "transitional," it should be seen as an "experimental society"*. It would always be in transition.

* * *

The anarchist method of an experimental society has broader application than economics. The oppression of women has been deeply rooted in historical society, always intertwined with various forms of class exploitation. It has been bound up with the way society raises its children, with the way we are all socialized, and with the personal identities we develop, as "men" and "women." Any revolution will have to involve the most oppressed of the working class, and of all society. Otherwise it will fail. Even if a revolution were to magically happen without mobilizing the women, it would rapidly degenerate back into class society unless women were thoroughly involved in every area of change. (Even Stalinist and nationalist revolutions have mobilized the women of their countries, although the status of women tended to fall back after the new rulers took over.)

The overthrow of capitalism will bring the end of the capitalist class as a class. The overthrow of sexist patriarchy will not require the abolition of men but the creation of new relationships between men and women. How will people carry out sexual/romantic love? How will they mate and raise children? We do not have answers to these questions. There will be a free society in which women are not economically dependent on men. Women will be free to develop their potentialities to the fullest. The community will take ultimate responsibility for all children, rather than make their mothers (or even their fathers) financially tied down. Beyond that, it will be up to the women and men of that society to find their own ways of loving and relating.

This will be a society based on voluntary association and free cooperation. Economically independent women will be able to assert their freedom and fight for their rights against male privilege. They can ally with men who are also committed to women's liberation. All other forms of sexism and gender stereotyping will be ended, through struggle, including the oppression of Gay men, Lesbians, Bisexuals, and Transgendered people. Democratic communities will be laboratories in which to work out new, freer, relations between the genders, and to reconsider what people mean by being male, or female, attracted to the same or different genders, or whatever they want to be.

* * *

The relations among the so-called races (nationalities, ethnic groups, whatever) will be reworked by a free people--using anarchy as an experimental method. It is impossible for there to be a revolution in the U.S. which does not mobilize the most oppressed sections of the working class, particularly African-Americans, Latinos, Asian-Americans, Native Americans, and other People of Color. A North American revolution must involve the whole multiracial, multinational, multilingual, working class, with leading positions being played by the most oppressed people. It will not only end poverty, slums, deadening unemployment and dead-end employment. The anti-authoritarian revolution will make it possible for oppressed racial and national groupings to organize themselves anyway they want. It will be essential that they do so, if the revolution is not to fall back into the old repressive society. Without a continuing battle against all forms of racism and white privilege, the old hierarchies will reappear, including classes and exploitation.

If enough African-Americans want to separate out into their own federation of distinct communities, they will be able to do that. (Under a stateless society, there will no longer be a national state to secede from.) Those African-Americans who want to be fully assimilated into the dominant culture will be able to do that--with the support of all the antiracist people of society. Perhaps many will want to maintain some separate "racial" organizations while sharing all the rights of the rest of society. That too, will be possible, in a federated, pluralistic, and experimental society. The same is true for other People of Color, such as Mexican-Americans, who might want to form their own communal federation in the former Southwestern U.S., for example.

Chapter 8. A World Without the State

It may be charged that these are European, Western, ideas, thought up by Dead White Men, and not relevant to most of the world. It is true that anarchism and Marxism were first developed in Europe. So were most modern political ideas, because capitalism and its industrialism first broke out in Europe, before it overran the world. Ideas first developed in Europe also included nationalism, democracy, and working class struggle. These are not European ideas, they are human ideas. There are incipient versions of these ideas in every culture. Every people has both reactionary and libertarian-democratic aspects to its culture. This must be so because each people has a history of class, national, and gender oppression, which includes a history of resistance to these oppressions. As capitalist industrialism spreads over the globe, people look for ways to resist, taking concepts from the first who suffered it in Europe, but combining them with their own traditions and making the concepts their own. So it is with libertarian socialism.

Today anarchism has spread over the globe. There are anarchists throughout Latin America again, as there were in the late 1900s and early twentieth century (the statist Sandinistas of Nicaragua used the colors red and black, because these were the colors of the labor movement which had once been initiated by anarchist-syndicalists). There are anarchists throughout Africa (Mbah & Igariwey, 1997), and in Korea, Japan, and even China and in the Middle East. There are anarchists in the Asiatic parts of the former Soviet Union. Marxism has been much discredited and people throughout the world are looking for an alternative way to be radical. With the new globalization of capitalism, there is an international working class in a way there has never been before. Throughout the poorer nations, an industrial proletariat has been created. We live in a new international world, where the world market is ever tighter and closer through computer connections and faster travel. The historic ideals of international proletarian revolution is more relevant than ever to the workers of the world.

* * *

Perhaps a final argument for statism is the supposed need for a centralized *world government*. This is not a call for various international organizations in specialized areas (such as UNICEF or bodies coordinating trade) nor for voluntary international federations (on the model of the UN, but without states). Anarchists, as internationalists and opponents of the nation state, have no problem with these. A world government means an international state with its own military and police forces, capable of ruling the world. It would be a monstrous bureaucratic nightmare. There are various arguments for its supposed necessity.

One argument is that world government is needed to abolish war. As national governments stopped wars between city-states, it is argued, so an international state is needed to stop wars between nations. However, it is not government which stopped local wars, it is the extent of economic and social integration which produced unified nations and their governments. So long as a nation is not unified, it could still have wars, which were called civil wars (or wars of national liberation or revolutionary wars). One of the bloodiest wars in history was the U.S. Civil War. Having a national government did not prevent it and having an international government would not prevent international "civil wars."

What is needed is the abolition of national oppression, dog-eat-dog international capitalist competition, imperialism, and the national states which serve the interests of the ruling corporate rich. Wars are due to the drives for national domination and exploitation which are built into the competitive system of capitalist national states. In a cooperative world without states, there would be no need for wars. National states exist to wage wars in the interest of their ruling classes. That is a major, if not the only, reason for their being. To keep the existing states but to pile another, larger, stronger, state on top of them all, is a formula for more wars, not fewer.

Another argument for world government rests on the supposed need for centralized international economic planning by a socialist system (as was raised by Bukharin, 1981). Factories in southern Africa and in Greenland would be managed from the same center in, say, Geneva. What inefficiency! This accepts the present overcentralization of the world economy which has been created by modern-day imperialist capitalism--for its own reasons. Women are hired by U.S. corporations to sew clothes in Bangladesh, but not because U.S. people cannot sew. It is cheaper to hire the Bangladeshis, that is all. Instead, anti-authoritarian socialists would argue that people can provide themselves with their necessary food, energy, clothing, shelter, and industry on the bases of their regions or clusters of regions. At the least, each continent, surely, has the necessary resources to provide for its people. There would still be exchange among the world's regions, in both goods and ideas. Because these would be a small part of the economy, they can be managed by trade commissions and limited international agencies.

* * *

The far-left raises another argument for world government. Even after a world revolution, for an indefinite period there will still be rich nations (the formerly imperialist countries) and poor nations (the formerly exploited nations, that is, most of the world). It is sometimes asserted that a world state will be needed to force the rich countries to share their wealth with the poorer lands, until all peoples are equal. A Trotskyist argues that "an anarcho-commune in upper Manhattan and one in a peasant village in India" will not be equal. Therefore there needs to be "an internationally planned, socialized economy with a central political government" (Seymour, 2001, p. 7). The same argument is made by a leading Maoist, who argues that, without an international dictatorship, anarchist communes in the former imperialist countries would only be " 'communizing' the plunder and exploitation that had been carried out by imperialism" (Avakian, 1997p. 3). While pointing to a real issue, this program is an awful idea, because it means a worldwide revolutionary dictatorship. A world "proletarian" dictatorship over North America, Western Europe, and Japan, will not be a workers' democracy in, say, Africa and the West Indies . The proposed international totalitarian state will rule over them too.

The main thing a North American/European revolution would do for the "Third World" is to get off its back. It would be a great boon for Asian, African, and Latin American development if Western nations just stopped engaging in the unfair trade, unequal investments, and ruinous loans by which they suck dry the oppressed nations. Merely canceling the international debts of the poorer peoples to the businesses and governments of the rich nations would be a huge gain. "Allowing" poor peoples to use the advanced technology and scientific ideas of the industrialized nations, without making them pay for international copyrights, would also be of great benefit.

Aside from this negative benefit from the formerly imperialist countries, the richer countries should find ways to help the poorer ones "industrialize" in their own way. A people which has freed itself by creating anti-authoritarian socialism would likely have a great deal of idealism, a desire to help others. This does not mean that they would be willing to beggar themselves or see their children starve. But the end of capitalist waste and the massive expenditures of military production will create a huge surplus of wealth to be used for many purposes.

At the same time, it will be in the self-interest of the richer countries to help the poorer ones. There can be no socialist utopia in North America and Europe which is surrounded by an ocean of world poverty. Poverty causes instability and lays the basis for a revival of class society in much of the world. The suffering of the poorer peoples lays the basis for the rise of reactionary and obscurantist ideologies (nationalist or religious fundamentalist or Stalinist). It would lead to wars among the poor nations, which will draw in the rich ones. It results in waves of immigration from the poor to the the rich countries, making it difficult for the rich countries to develop ecological balance between population and the environment (which is not a justification for attempts to limit immigration by state-enforced borders, now or in the future). In short, the former imperialist countries will help the poorer nations because it is in their interest to do so.

As mentioned, much practical decentralist technology was first developed as instruments for helping the poorer nations develop in their own way (Schumacher, 1973; McRobie, 1981). "Industrializing" these peoples with huge dams, monstrous factories, cities with skyscrapers, and up-to-the-minute airports only pleases their new rulers, the national bourgeoisie and statesmen (and deepens their debt to Western banks). Instead, Western libertarian socialist countries could provide the capital for an intermediate technology, developed together with local people, ecologically balanced and permitting a democratic transition out of poverty. Decentralism does not contradict world development--it is a precondition for it.

All over the world, people work and slave to take care of themselves and those they love. But over them all is the capitalist class which drains them of their wealth and productivity. Holding together the capitalist class, everywhere and always, is the state, with its army, police, officials, bureaucrats, courts, tax collectors, and politicians. All peoples are capable of getting rid of this monstrous domination. Freedom and self-management are for the whole world.

PART II: State and Revolution... and Counterrevolution

CHAPTER 9: THE RUSSIAN REVOLUTION

Discussing the nature of the state and the possibilities of replacing it may seem like abstract theory. Yet *this concept of the state was developed through the experience of popular revolutions, when the revolutionary people taught the political theorists.* Marx and Engels, and the early anarchists, lived through the experience of the European-wide revolution of 1848 and then the Paris Commune of 1871. Later Marxists and anarchists participated in the Russian revolutions of 1905 and 1917 and the following European revolutions after World War I, which shook the whole world. In turn, revolutions have succeeded or failed (mostly failed) according to the understanding of the state by revolutionary activists. Revolutionaries study revolutions. We need to know how they have happened, how they succeeded, how they have failed, and how they have been betrayed.

In the midst of our daily, nonrevolutionary existence, it is inspiring to see how revolutions have broken out, how ordinary people have risen up to throw out their oppressors, and how millions of people have sought, if only for a time, to create societies without the state. The greatest benefit of many revolutions has been the example of the people rising up, and trying to transform their lives into freedom. In particular, it is highly valuable to study two revolutions in which anarchists participated, in which popular struggles produced creative forms of freedom, even if they ended in defeat. To most historians, the story of revolutions is the account of replacing the old state with a new state. To anarchists, the most interesting story is how working people threw out the old rulers and organized themselves to run society in a "festival of liberation." The establishment of the new state is the counterrevolution.

I will review two world-shaking revolutions, which can stand as templates for other upheavals: the 1917-21 Russian revolution and the 1936-39 Spanish revolution and also a world-shaking nonrevolutionary struggle, the German fight against fascism in the early thirties.

* * *

The Russian revolution (Avrich, 1973; Deutscher, 1954; Farber, 1990; Hobson & Tabor, 1988; Pipes, 1990; Rabinowitch, 1968, 1976; Sirianni, 1982; Tabor, 1988; Trotsky, 1967) began in the winter of 1917, in February--actually it was in March, but the Russians were then using an old-fashioned calendar which was two weeks behind the rest of Europe. (It is also important to note that there had been an earlier Russian revolution, in 1905. It had been defeated, but it laid the basis for the 1917 revolution.) The revolution began on International Women's Day as a demonstration by working class women in one of the two major Russian cities, Petrograd (or St. Petersburg, later Leningrad, now Petrograd again; the other major city being Moscow). The socialist parties urged the women to wait for a better time, but they were hungry, their families were hungry, and they were angry. Their demonstration became a rebellion which quickly spread to the male workers throughout the city and then to soldiers and to the peasants in nearby regions.

At that time, the Russian empire combined a backward, semi-feudal, mostly peasant country, run by an unchecked king (Czar or Tsar), with the most modern type of industries, huge factories, established by international capitalism. This awkward, inefficient system was strained by three years of World War I. The poorly organized, inefficient, Russian army, top-heavy with ignorant, feudal-minded officers, and with illiterate peasant soldiers at the base, had to face the well-organized German army, backed by its highly industrialized economy.

Since 1914, the Russian army and the Russian economy had been under incredible strain and were in a state of virtual collapse. Unable to provide adequate food, clothing, ammunition, or transportation to its armed forces, the empire kept its exhausted men in the war at the insistence of the British and French capitalist governments. Finally the Russian army rebelled, deserted by the thousands, refused to go on the offensive, mutinied, fraternized with German soldiers, and occasionally shot officers. Mutiny in the military plus the workers' rebellion forced the Czar to abdicate.

The urban rebellion gathered steam in waves of strikes and factory occupations. The workers held assemblies of everyone in the factory or department and elected committees to make sure that production continued. At the same time they elected delegates to districtwide and citywide councils.

The Russian word for "council" is *soviet*. The workers remembered how they had created soviets in the attempted 1905 revolution. Originally the soviets/councils were seen as merely strike committees, but they began to take over the functions of a semi-government. The police had been driven from the streets and from their station houses--security was taken over by squads of armed workers from the factories. Workers in the telephone exchange or railroads or printing plants or anywhere else would not obey "official" orders without the endorsement of the soviet's elected executive committee. The soviets were representative bodies, but far more democratic than any parliament. Rooted in the workplaces, their delegates could be recalled by new elections; the delegates were, by definition, from the working class, and had little chance for personal corruption.

However, their very democratic looseness created certain weaknesses in the soviets. They were conventions of people who had never had a chance to be heard and they were places for talking and speeches. Therefore they were vulnerable to being dominated in fact by small groups of intellectuals (party officials) who formed the executive committees which carried out the actual work. They were also vulnerable to being packed. Finally, as representative bodies, although more reflective of the ranks than capitalist parliaments, there was still a lag time between changes in the opinions of the workers and changes in their delegates (and the executive committees elected by the delegates). The limitations of the soviets would have been greatly reduced by making sure delegates were chosen and watched over by popular assemblies (in the workplace or neighborhoods). But none of the political parties was interested in that.

The revolution spread. Soldiers and sailors held assemblies, elected committees, and sent delegates to their own soviets, which affiliated with the workers' soviets (the workers were very aware how important it was to get the soldiers on their side). By the Fall, there were about 900 soviets throughout the country. These were more-or-less affiliated with each other. The first All-Russian Congress (Soviet) of Workers', Soldiers', and Peasants' Deputies was held in Petrograd on June 1917. The Second was in October.

The workers' factory committees began by checking the capitalists and management, to make sure they were not sabotaging production--the Russian term for "workers' control" meant only "supervision." But over time the workers began to take over factories and run them themselves-- which in Russian was referred to as "workers' management." They set up committees to contact peasants or other industries to get raw materials; they made sure production was carried out; they had boards to ensure that proper discipline was maintained in the plant; they established wage schedules; they made contact with either central authorities or other plants to get their product distributed. They began to call for their plants to be "nationalized"--not meaning run by the state, but that the plants should be taken away from the capitalists, socially owned, and managed by the workers (including white-collar clerks and engineers).

How efficient was worker managed production, in 1917 and after, has been hotly debated (Avrich, 1973; Sirianni, 1982). The Russian economy had been falling apart before the revolution even began--this was a cause of the revolution. Of course, the workers were inexperienced and made mistakes. Much depended, in each workplace, on their ability to get the white collar workers, the specialists, to continue working.

But the capitalists and pro-capitalist managers persistently sabotaged production, faced with even the lightest of worker organization. This made workers' management necessary but difficult. Overall, in spite of many obstacles, worker-managed factories did seem to improve production (Sirianni, 1982).

Most importantly, the peasants began to rebel (of course, the big majority of the soldiers were peasants, since most of the country was so rural and undeveloped). They too formed committees, met in village assemblies (often reviving the traditional all-male village assemblies), and divided up the land. They broke into manor houses as well as barns, divided up the furniture and livestock, and often burned down the gentry's' buildings as they did so. This rural revolution was slow to spread, but when it did, the peasants were thorough about it, finishing off feudal landlordism for good.

Cooperatives spread throughout the country. Consumer cooperatives grew in the cities and both consumer and marketing coops in the countryside, to help peasants buy and sell in bulk without the middleman merchant. At the time, the Bolsheviks sneered at the cooperatives, as a middle-class and rich-peasant matter. Near the end of his life, Lenin was to praise the cooperatives as an essential element in building socialism which had been often overlooked by the Bolsheviks (see "On Cooperation," in Lenin, 1971; Buber, 1958).

The mighty Russian empire began to come apart at the seams. Once called "the prisonhouse of nations," its oppressed nations and minorities--Poles, Ukrainians, Georgians, Jews, Kazakhs, and others, over half the population of imperial Russia--began to demand independence or at least autonomy. They set up local governments and began to run things in their own languages, instead of the Russian they had been forced to use for so long.

The political parties had not organized the February revolution, nor invented the soviets or the popular assemblies, committees, and councils. Even the most revolutionary of parties lagged behind the people, advising against the initial strikes and demonstrations or the popular forms of struggle. In part it was no fault of theirs that the parties were caught behind the masses. For 12 years (since 1905), they had been advocating revolution of some sort, while the people in their majority had been unresponsive and nonrevolutionary. Then the socialist parties had been ahead of the working people--organizing small groups, "patiently explaining" their ideas (to use Lenin's terms). When the people broke out in revolution, the parties were still in their years-long pattern of "patiently explaining." Inevitably, it took a while for the parties to reorient themselves to a suddenly and radically changed situation.

However, it was also true that the parties' centralism and conservatism played a part in their lagging behind the people. For example, when the soviets were first created in 1905, the Bolshevik party called on them to disband because they were not under its control. Furthermore, both the Leninist Bolsheviks and the more moderate Mensheviks--the two Marxist parties--were in theory and program against a socialist revolution. They believed that all societies had to go through a series of "stages," and that, since Russia was still semi-feudal, it had to go through a capitalist-democratic revolution before it was ready for a socialist revolution. Therefore they were unprepared to deal with popular actions which went beyond the limits of capitalism--such as workers' seizure of factories and establishing socialized production.

The February revolution has often been called a "spontaneous" revolution. This is based on the elitist concept that if a revolution is not planned by some party then it is nonconscious, irrational, and sort of a natural process. In fact the people were quite aware of what they were doing and did it well. Leadership was provided by ordinary people, many of whom were rank-and-file members of the socialist parties or had been listening for years to the parties' propaganda. Taking courage from one another, despairing of change from above, and relying on ideas they had been hearing for years, they dared to hope and to act. They overthrew a centuries-old monarchy, they established popular-democratic organizations throughout the country, they began to seize the factories, and they inaugurated a peasant war for the land.

* * *

Yet the result was not a new society. After the February revolution, the Czar was gone but the capitalists and landlords remained. The army remained and the war remained. In place of the Czar was a new state, the Provisional Government (originally a committee of the old, Czarist, Duma, a powerless council elected on a very limited basis). Composed of pro-capitalist and monarchist politicians, it relied on the old governmental bureaucracy, the military officer corps, and the banks and big business. It was allied with the Western European imperialist governments which demanded the continuation of the war. As we shall see, it was this capitalist-bureaucratic-imperialist state machine which laid the basis for the Communist state.

In effect, Russia had two governments--or semi-governments. This was called "dyarchy" or *"dual power."* There was the official Provisional Government, which had little popular support. It continued to exist mainly because the reformist socialist leaders of the soviets supported it. On the other hand, there was the soviets, which had the popular support, including of the soldiers and armed workers, that is, of whatever armed force there was. But the majority in the the soviets supported the reformist socialists, who in turn gave their support to the Provisional Government.

The problem lay with two interrelated forces, the people and the political parties. The working people (2 to 5 percent were urban workers, the rest were peasants) combined the most advanced thinking with the most backward prejudices. They wanted freedom but they also looked to leaders to think for them. They wanted socialism but they also wanted private property (actually the peasants wanted social ownership of the land but division into small family plots). They wanted the war to end, but they were patriotic (patriotism claims a common interest between the mass of people and the ruling minority). They wanted a rational reorganization of society but they were steeped in religious superstition as well as anti-Semitism. They chose representatives (to the soviets and other bodies) from the socialist parties, but they knew little about the differences among the parties--at least at first.

The political parties were crystalized out of the various classes. They combined the best of popular consciousness--the desire for democracy, freedom, and socialism--with the worst--the desire for someone to be the boss. Although they educated people in new ideas, ultimately they rode the people's backwardness.

Of the political parties, some were explicitly pro-capitalist. To the reformist Marxists (the Mensheviks), these parties should have led the revolution against the semi-feudal Czarist system. In fact, they could not. The capitalists had too many ties to the feudal forces, such as loans to the landlords and other business deals. And the capitalists feared the uprising of the peasants, because it would redistribute property and, therefore, inspire their workers to similarly seize the capitalists' property. Furthermore, Russian capitalists were also tied by loans, investments and culture to European capitalism--and while Russia may have been backward overall, Europe as a whole was ripe for a socialist revolution.

So the capitalists' liberal parties, which had seemed so rebellious in the days of the Czar, quickly became conservative once the February revolution had occurred. The landlords, the monarchists, and the most rabid anti-Semites on the right merged with the pro-capitalist liberals into one reactionary bloc, represented by the Cadet (Constitutional Democrat) Party. At first, these constituted the Provisional Government but their popular base was in the upper classes. They had little support in the soviets, which were, after all, mostly representative of workers and peasants.

Instead the popular forces supported the socialist parties, of which there were three main ones. The largest was the Socialist Revolutionary ("SR") Party. Rather than being Marxist, it was "populist" ("Narodnik"). This was an amorphous ideology, which believed in the power of the people to change society, without emphasizing the urban working class. It claimed that the peasants' associations could develop directly into socialism. Its activists were important in building cooperatives.

Historically, populist activists had been bomb throwers and assassins of the royalty, to no great effect. Their strategy was vague and the SR membership ranged from people on the right who were little more than vague liberals (such as Alexander Kerensky) to leftists who were close to being socialist anarchists (the Maximalists). The SR's very vagueness left them open to all sorts of mildly liberal opportunists who wanted to be popular. Their pro-peasant stance, as well as their programmatic vagueness, made them the largest party in a time when most working people had little idea of the differences among the socialists.

The next largest left party was the Mensheviks--the reformist Social Democrats. Of the two Marxist parties, they were the most right wing, or, if you prefer, moderate. As already mentioned, their ideology declared that Russia was going through a capitalist revolution, preparing the way for further capitalist development, and that the capitalist politicians should be leading things. They believed in a "two-stage revolution." First a capitalist one, then someday a socialist one. Completely unrealistically, they expected to be organizing unions and an opposition social democratic party in a democratic parliament. They did not want to smash the bourgeois state, but to build it. Having a harder program than the SRs, they dominated their larger partner.

I have referred to the Mensheviks and the right SRs as "reformist" because they were opposed to a revolution against capitalism. However, they had supported the revolution against Czarism, and struggled for it for many years. Internationally they tended to identify with those on the center-left of the social democratic movement: those who spoke of revolution but acted in a waffling, semi-reformist, fashion. They were socialists of the center and are most precisely called *"centrists."*

The other Marxist party was the Bolsheviks, led by Lenin. (Under his urging they were to drop the names "Bolshevik" and "Social Democrat" in favor of "Communist," which they have used ever since.) For years they too had expected the revolution to be a capitalist-democratic one, opening up a period of capitalist development. Unlike the Mensheviks, they did not expect the capitalists or capitalist parties to be able to carry this out, for the reasons just mentioned. The revolution would be led by the workers' party in cooperation with a peasant party. But like the Mensheviks, they expected it to stay within the boundaries of capitalism. They too expected to build a bourgeois state. This was a modified version of a "two-stage revolution."

Trotsky had been almost the only Marxist to expect that a revolution in Russia would have to go beyond the bounds of liberal capitalism; that is, that the workers would seize the factories and the state would have to nationalize industry; and that the Russian revolution would have to spread to Europe if it were to survive (his theory of "permanent revolution"). However, by 1917 Lenin had come to the conclusion that the revolution would go over into socialist policies. He still thought that Russia, by itself, was too backward to skip over a capitalist stage, but now he considered a Russian revolution as part of the international (or at least European) revolution. Lenin persuaded the Bolshevik party to his point of view. (And Trotsky joined Lenin's party.)

Note that none of the Russian Marxist parties had planned for a socialist revolution. There had been no discussion of how socialism would be organized (Tabor, 1988), how the workers might manage industry (Sirianni, 1982), how the peasants might be peacefully brought to collectivize agriculture, and so on. Not that this would necessarily have made a difference, considering the centralized image Marxists held of socialism, but it might have.

Smallest of the main Russian political tendencies were the anarchists (Avrich, 1973). Their great theoretician, Peter Kroptkin, had returned to Russia, but he was discredited among the most radical for his support for the imperialist war. Unlike the parties, the anarchists did not have existing organizations or press before the February revolution. As soon as possible, they created federations, at least in the two main cities. They were as torn by factionalism as the Marxists, including differences between anti-organizational individualists, Kropotkinian communist-anarchists (who emphasized building communes), and anarchist-syndicalists (who emphasized work in industry, advocating workers' management). The anarchist-syndicalists were more pro-organizational and they developed a following among workers well out of proportion to their numbers. They participated in the soviets, while recognizing their limitations. Although anarchists played a significant role in the revolution (as we shall see), they never caught up to the Bolsheviks in size or influence, except in Ukraine.

Faced with the weakness of the liberal Cadet party and its government, the centrist/reformist socialists dared not let them fail. Then they would have had to take responsibility. Against their better judgment, the socialists joined the capitalist government to keep it afloat. This was an early example of what came to be called "Popular Front" governments: coalitions of liberal capitalist and reform socialist parties. Coalition with the capitalist parties served as an excuse for the socialists to not carry out socialist policies, while the capitalists forced the socialists to share the blame for capitalist policies.

Nor did the government of liberals and socialists carry out even liberal democratic policies. They did not call elections for a founding parliament ("Constituent Assembly"), nor give the landlords' lands to the peasants, nor offer self-determination to oppressed nationalities, nor limit the working day to eight hours. Nor did they end the war (instead they organized new military "offenses" that gained nothing but killed many Russian soldiers). They did little except keep the rotting structure wobbling on, solving nothing, and settling nothing.

In the months between February and October, the population began to shift to the revolutionary left (with ups and downs). The Bolsheviks grew in numbers and influence. So did the anarchists, which worried the Bolsheviks. The left wing of the Socialist Revolutionaries grew to such an extent that it finally split the party.

Of the three socialist parties, the Bolsheviks alone completely rejected the capitalist Provisional Government. They saw the soviets as an alternate state power. Lenin realized that the soviets could be the vehicle to bring his party to power (the Mensheviks repeatedly denounced him as an "anarchist" for this). His program, as expressed in many documents, such as *The Impending Catastrophe and How to Combat it* (Lenin, 1970b, pp. 237--275), was a contradiction. He called for the centralization of the economy on the model of the

German imperialist war economy, with its compulsory monopolization of major industries under the coordination of the military state. But he wanted this centralized economy to be managed and supervised by the workers' organizations: soviets, factory committees, and unions. He did not see the contradiction between the decentralized, federalist, nature of the soviets and workplace committees, and the model of a centralized, state-monopolized (but still capitalist) economy.

When the Communists had enough popular support, they organized a military uprising. It dispersed the Provisional Government and handed power over to the All-Russian Congress of Soviets in which the Communists and their allies had a majority. This was the *October revolution*. Culminating months of mass struggle, it had majority support--not for the rule of the Communists but for the soviets to replace the Provisional Government.

As mentioned earlier, *it is not often realized the extent to which the October revolution--and the early soviet government--was a coalition effort, a united front.* The Bolsheviks themselves had drawn other left socialists into their ranks, despite historical differences--the most important group being that around Trotsky. The military rebellion was organized with the support of the Left Social Revolutionaries (which had recently formed into their own party). Lenin's agrarian decree for the new regime was a straight steal from the SR program. The Left SRs joined the Communists as junior partners in a coalition soviet government, with personnel in all soviet agencies, even the Cheka (the new secret police).

The anarchists had generally been in agreement with the Communists in their agitation against the Provisional Government. (But they were ambivalent about the slogan "All power to the soviets!" since this could be interpreted in an authoritarian direction.) They participated in the October insurrection--there were at least four anarchists in the the military committee which organized it. An anarchist sailor led the military force which dispersed the Constituent Assembly after it refused to recognize the soviet authority (anarchists rejected a parliament anyway). Anarchists delegates mostly voted with the Communists in the soviets. They saw themselves as supporting the Communist-Left SR coalition, with criticisms. The anarchists were in a de facto coalition with the regime.

However, the Bolsheviks had no interest in maintaining the coalition. Lenin had been opposed to it from the start. This was in spite of the fact that , without the Left SRs, the Communists had almost no base in the countryside. Instead they created a break with the Left SRs partly by their virtual war against the peasants, when the cities and army ran out of grain. The Bolshevik response was to send outsiders to seize the peasants' grain, based on unrealistic and dogmatic theories of class conflict in the village and a generally authoritarian outlook (Sirianni, 1982). A more reasonable policy, relying on the peasant soviets to collect taxes while otherwise permitting a market in grain, would have fed more people and perhaps kept the coalition going.

The other reason for the split with the Left SRs was the Communist approval of the humiliating peace treaty of Brest Litovsk with the Germans. This gave up a great deal of the Russian peoples to the Germans, including all of the Ukrainians. Lenin rammed this through the Communist party, over the protests of the Left Communist faction (then led by Nicholas Bukharin), which probably had a majority on this issue (Trotsky voted for the treaty, not because he thought it was right but because he did not want a split with Lenin).

The Left SRs and Left Communists advocated a revolutionary war, at least in part a guerrilla war. The very war-weariness of the Russian peoples, they argued, meant that a new, revolutionary, army could only be built in the heat of waging a revolutionary war against a foreign invader and counterrevolutionary armies (which is how the Red Army was actually to be built). Given the actual weakness of the Germans (who were soon to lose World War I), the anti-treaty forces may have been realistic. This has been argued by Isaac Deutscher (1954), Trotsky's biographer, as well as by Pipes (1990), the conservative historian.

However, Lenin felt strongly about this (as he did about most things). By threats of resigning, he blackmailed the party leadership into backing him and overrode the majority of his own party. All accounts of the discussions among the Bolsheviks show a complete lack of concern that this might drive the Left SRs out of the coalition. Yet with only one party in the soviets, they were inevitably to become lifeless, mere extensions of the party-state.

The anarchists also denounced the treaty. The Fourth Congress of Soviets was called to vote on the treaty in March, 1918. All fourteen anarchist delegates voted against it. Soon the anarchists were being suppressed. On April 11, the Cheka raided 26 Moscow anarchist centers. Over five hundred anarchists were arrested and more than 40 killed or wounded. This coalition was over. However most anarchists continued to support the Communists against the White right-wing armies in the Russian civil war. (So did most Mensheviks, incidentally.)

The anarchists played a major role in Ukrainian resistance to the White armies when Nestor Makhno successfully organized a national guerrilla army (Skirda, 2004). As mentioned, it defeated two White armies and held off the Russian Red Army. Anarchist activists organized an educational and propaganda arm of the guerrilla force. They built up a system of free soviets, uncontrolled by the Communists. Twice Makhno's forces made alliances with the Communist regime to fight the foreign invaders and the White counterrevolutionaries. Finally the Red Army crushed the popular forces by treachery, mass arrests and killing, supported by vicious lies. Makhno was one of a few leaders who escaped to Western Europe.

In June 1918, the Left SRs rebelled against the Communists, not to overthrow them but to change their policies. It is possible that they could have seized power (in the opinion of Pipes, 1990). There was already much dissatisfaction with the Communists, and the Left SRs had people spread throughout industry and the local armed forces. But as libertarians they did not want power--and so they left the Communists with it. The Communists were not shy about using power. Soon the leading Left SRs were in jail. Had the Left SRs instead seized power, in order to immediately call for new elections to the soviets, with free discussion at least among left parties, the history of Russia might have been different.

By 1921 the civil wars were mostly over. The sailors of the fortress "Kronstadt," which guarded Petrograd, mutinied. They demanded the revival of the multi-tendency democracy of the soviets, and easing up on the peasants. Anarchists and even local Communists were involved in the rebellion. The government sent military forces to crush the sailors, massacring captured sailors, and publicly lying that they were agents of counterrevolutionary White forces.

Soon afterwards, the Communists did ease up on the peasants, making it possible for them to trade more freely. The whole economy was opened up to more capitalist measures (the New Economic Policy, called by Lenin, "state capitalism"). However, there were no efforts to permit or encourage worker-run cooperatives.

To balance this economic opening, the party reinforced its outlawry of all other parties, and then outlawed opposition factions within the one party. The legal framework for totalitarian state capitalism was now set. Within two more years, Lenin was dead of an illness and Trotsky had been expelled from the party as a Left Oppositionist. Stalin and Bukharin (now on the Right) were dominant, with a program of encouraging the peasantry. By 1929, Stalin had politically crushed Bukharin and was now the unlimited dictator. He began the policy of forcibly collectivizing the peasantry, killing thousands. He forcibly built an industrial economy by state coercion (almost enslavement) of the workers, killing more thousands. In the late thirties he began the vast purge campaigns, imprisoning and murdering millions, pressing the bureaucracy into shape as a new ruling class. Overall, Stalin killed all the remaining members of Lenin's Central Committee (including Trotsky and Bukharin), almost all the living members of the original Bolshevik party cadre, and millions of workers and peasants. Estimates range beyond twenty million people killed. Also murdered was the ideal of communism.

* * *

Significant parts of the pattern of the Russian revolution have been repeated over and over again, in revolution after revolution:

(1) The emergence of popular councils, workplace committees, peasant unions, cooperatives, neighborhood assemblies and other mass democratic organizations. These stand as alternatives to both the old state and to a new, centralized state, in a situation of dual power. They raise the possibility of a nonstate solution to the crisis.

(2) The waffling of the liberals. The openly pro-capitalist liberals are unable to break with the conservative forces due to their ties to the basically reactionary system of capitalism. They are champions of the bourgeois state, however much they may criticize.

(3) The waffling of the moderate socialists (reformists as well as pseudo-revolutionary centrists). They are unable or unwilling to break with the liberals. Actually "waffling" is too nice a way of saying it. The liberals and socialists repeatedly betray their followers by capitulating to right-wing forces. They reject the idea of smashing the state.

(4) The drive of the Communists or nationalists to create a new, centralized, state (in some variant of state capitalism). However, this does not simply follow the Russian pattern. After 1917, the Communists never again rode to power on the backs of soviet-like democratic councils. From then on, Communists only came to power on the backs of nonproletarian armies (the Russian army in most of Eastern Europe, the peasant-based Chinese People's Army, similar forces in Yugoslavia and Vietnam, etc.). When they did not have an army at hand, instead, the Communists acted like waffling reformists. Better a traditional capitalist state than a workers' council system! This change is one piece of evidence that the original Leninism had transmuted into something new. The Maoists developed a new version of the "two stage strategy." First a bourgeois state, then someday socialism. But-- what was new--was that the Communist Party would control the state from the beginning, even in the bourgeois stage (now called "New Democracy"). "Socialism" then meant that the Communist Party-controlled bourgeois state would, at some time, nationalize industry, as it did. When industry is nationalized by a bourgeois state, this is, by

definition, state capitalism, and sometimes they admit this. This system made it possible for the state to eventually decide to denationalize (privatize) industries, while maintaining the party dictatorship, as in today's China.

(5) The anarchists are poorly organized and unprepared. A number of Russian anarchists, including Nester Makhno (Makhno et al.,1989) came to the conclusion that anarchists need to be more coordinated and self-disciplined if they are to seriously compete with Communists and others. As Gregrory Maksimov concluded by September 1918, "We anarchists and syndicalists...we were too disorganized, too weak, and so we have allowed this to happen" (in Avrich, 1973, pp. 124-125). I would add that anarchists need theory, strategy, and a willingness to be flexible in their tactics. In the Russian revolution they were wildly outmaneuvered by Lenin, a genius at tactics. This led Makno and others in exile to develop a program (the "Platform") for anarchists to form an organization to fight for anarchism by democratically developing unity of action and program.

* * *

From the start, Lenin, Trotsky, and the rest of the Bolsheviks had argued that the revolution would succeed only if it spread to Western Europe. And revolutions did break out in Europe, including a toppling of the German monarchy by workers' councils, the mutiny of half the French army, the outbreak of workers' councils in northern Italy, and "soviet republics" declared in Hungary and in Bohemia. But these were all defeated, to a great extent by the betrayals of the reformist and centrist socialists, and also by the inexperience of the revolutionary left. Yet the imperialist countries were too weak and divided to crush the new Russian state (although there were attempts, invasions and backing of the various Russian counterrevolutionary armies).

So the new Soviet Union was left dangling. The Communists were still in power but the country was devastated. It had gone through a world war, then a revolution, and finally a civil war. The industrial infrastructure was worn out. The working class was cut down to a quarter its original size. Famine existed in large parts of the country. The people were demoralized and depoliticized.

Much of this, anarchists argue, was the fault of the Leninists themselves. The war on the peasants drove the peasants to cut back production as well as to lose interest in politics. The failure to rely on the creativity of the workers made industry less productive. The abolition of all other parties--and then of all factions within the one ruling party--(all done under Lenin and Trotsky) increased the people's depoliticization. But the backwardness, poverty, and isolation of Russian after the revolution were real facts. They encouraged the authoritarian tendencies in Bolshevism. Given these problems, it may have been inevitable that the workers and peasants would lose power in Russia, either to an armed counterrevolution or to the "enemy within," the rise of a new class.

However, my study of Lenin over the years has led me to two conclusions (essentially the same as Taber, 1988; also see Hobson & Tabor, 1988). One is that Lenin did not intend to create a totalitarian state--as compared, for example, with Hitler, who knew what he was doing all along. Lenin really wanted what he regarded as the rule of the workers, and (unlike Stalin later) he very much wanted to spread it through international workers' revolution At the end of his life he was distressed at the extent of bureaucratism in the state and party, although he had no idea what to do about it except to reshuffle the system. His last political act, as he was dying, was to try to bloc with Trotsky to remove Stalin. It is also significant that there were repeated oppositions within the Bolshevik party to authoritarian policies, including Lenin's policies (the Left Communists, the Workers' Opposition, the Democratic Centralists), as well as to Stalin's later policies (the Left--or Trotskyist-- and Right--Bukharinist--Oppositions).

But my other conclusion is that Lenin and his party were authoritarian and laid the basis for Stalinist totalitarianism. (Each of those intraparty oppositions was defeated and virtually all their leaders, except Trotsky, capitulated to Stalin.) As I have argued, Lenin built his party on a program of centralism: centralization of the party, centralization of the state, and centralization of the economy. To him, the idea of industry run by workers' committees was only a step toward a topdown economy planned by experts. Like all Marxists, Lenin never had a conception of rooting socialism in local direct democracy. Similarly he advocated land to the the peasants, only as a transition toward centralized collectivism, and self-determination of minority nations only as a step toward a centralized multinational state. (There is nothing subtle about this analysis; Lenin's centralism was explicit in all his writings.)

Further, while Lenin had not advocated a one-party party-state before taking power, neither had he ever advocated a multiparty workers' democracy. For most of his political career, his model of the revolutionary state was the "revolutionary dictatorship of the proletariat and peasantry," a capitalist government run by radical parties, comparable to the Jacobin dictatorship of the French revolution.

There was supported by Lenin's belief in the absolute truth of Marxism and in *his* knowledge of this truth. With this revelation to guide him, he felt no doubts about the suppression of opponents or the the rightness of his course. Knowing he was right, he had no need to learn from other parties or to implement checks-and-balances in his state.

Finally, there is the strain of ruthlessness in Lenin's politics. He was so determined not to repeat the "softness" of previous revolutions which had failed that he was prepared to kill his political opponents without limits. He set up the Cheka, the first of the Communist secret police, with the power not only to investigate but to judge and punish (kill) without supervision. He outlawed other parties and even opposition within the Communist Party, and used the Cheka to enforce this one-party, one-faction, state. He waged war on the peasants. None of this is the same as Stalin, who murdered tens of millions of people (more than Hitler), but it was the outline of the Stalinist state.

Imagine if there had been a serious, well-organized, socialist-anarchist organization during the Russian revolution. As late as 1918, the Bolshevik party almost split over the unjust peace treaty (the Left

Communists were also more favorable to factory committees than Lenin's centralizer faction). The Left SRs came close to seizing power in their rebellion. A strong anarchist organization *might have* created a coalition with the Left Communists and Left SRs in the soviets which might have changed world history. Or again, in 1921, after the end of the civil war, much of the rural country was in revolt, Petrograd had a general strike, and the military fortress of Kronstadt mutinied under anarchist influence (Avrich, 1970). A national anarchist organization, had there been one, might have been able to coordinate a successful third revolution. Of course, I say "might", but the anarchists and populists could hardly have done worse than the Leninists.

CHAPTER 10. THE SPANISH REVOLUTION

As Maoists study the Chinese revolution, Fidelistas study the Cuban revolution, and Trotskyists study the Russian, so anarchists should study the Spanish revolution of 1936 to 1939 (see Bookchin, 1978; Brenan, 1971; Dolgoff, 1974; Guerin, 1970; Guillamon, 1996; Morrow, 1974; Orwell, 1980; Paz, 1976; Peirats, 1974; Radosh, Habeck, & Sevostianov, 2001; Richards, 1972; Trotsky, 1973; Woodcock, 1962). It was the last of the great working class upheavals after World War I and a precursor of World War II, and yet it remains highly relevant to today's struggles. The anarchists played an enormous role in the Spanish revolution. Half the working class was organized in their trade union federation (the CNT)--almost all the working class in the industrial center of Spain, the province of Catalonia. Much of the peasantry was anarchist-influenced. In the course of a great revolution, the anarchists showed their strengths: leading military forces, organizing collectivized farms, and creating worker-managed industries. Much of the anarchist literature on Spain has been celebratory, focusing on these real achievements.

Yet the Spanish anarchists also showed severe weaknesses in the course of the revolution. The leading anarchists felt it necessary to abandon their principles and program. They allied themselves with bourgeois and Stalinist parties, entered the capitalist government as ministers, and held back the workers and peasants from completing the revolution. Rather than smashing the state, they joined it. And they finally lost to the fascist army of Franco. Anarchists can be challenged--and quite rightly--"How do we know that anarchists will not repeat the same mistakes in another revolutionary situation?" This cannot be answered unless we know why they made these mistakes and how to avoid them in the future.

* * *

The Spanish revolution of 1936 to 1939 is often referred to as a "civil war." And while it *was* a civil war--a conflict within a country--this covers up the revolutionary aspect of it, the conflict *between classes* (this is similar to those historians who refer to the U.S. revolution as a "war for independence," for the same motive of denying that there was a revolution). Sometimes it is dated back to 1931, when King Alfonso (grandfather of the current Spanish king) abdicated and the republic was established. Five years of upheaval, rebellion, and mass strikes followed, which the government dealt with by severe repression. By January 1936, over 30 thousand workers and leftists were in prison.

In February, new elections threw out the conservative parties in favor of the Popular Front, a coalition of liberal capitalist ("Republican") parties and the Socialist Party. The organized anarchists did not endorse the Popular Front and were officially for boycotting the election. In practice they deliberately did not campaign for their position, accepting that most of the workers in the anarchist unions would vote for the Popular Front. Even those workers and peasants who had no illusions in the Popular Front still hoped that it would amnesty the tens of thousands of class war prisoners, as it promised In the four day period between the election and the inauguration, workers carried out the amnesty where they could by forcing open the jails!

Otherwise, the liberal/social democratic coalition was a typical do-nothing reformist regime, unable to break up the landed estates, to improve the conditions of the workers, to limit the power of the Catholic Church (subsidized by the government and politically very reactionary), or to clear out the fascists from the army officer corps. But it was still capable of using the police or military against the workers in the event of strikes or demonstrations. Nevertheless, the capitalist class found the Popular Front too weak for its purposes; a strong hand was needed to crush the working class.

In July 1936, the military rebelled, in alliance with traditional monarchists and with new fascist forces (the Falange). They had the support of almost all the Spanish bourgeoisie. Bringing over the bulk of the army from the Spanish colony of Morocco, General Francisco Franco and his allies hoped to quickly win a coup d'etat and establish a dictatorship. After all, Hitler had taken power in Germany in 1933 without resistance by the large German workers' parties (the Social Democrats and the Communists), let alone by the liberal democrats (see next chapter). The Popular Front government dithered, denied that there was a military rebellion and tried to make a deal with Franco. Almost all of the military and police went over to the fascists, leaving the official government floating in midair. The capitalists and the big landowners mostly abandoned their businesses and farms and supported Franco, leaving the capitalist politicians only as the "shadow of the bourgeoisie" (in Trotsky's phrase; Trotsky, 1973).

However, unlike Germany, the Spanish workers resisted. Almost unarmed, they frustrated the military rebellion. Barracks were encircled by masses of people who would not let the soldiers join the rebellion. The government refused to arm the workers (and even tried to forcibly disarm them). The people gathered up what weapons they had, took more from gun shops, and seized guns from the police and military. Miners brought their dynamite. Houses surrounding military barracks were set afire by gasoline. Fascist machine gun emplacements at street crossroads were taken out by automobiles driven at them at full speed. Unions organized volunteer forces (the militias) to go out and fight the army. Despite the waffling of the government, the workers and peasants prevented the fascists from winning an easy and quick victory. Instead they had to fight a three-year drawn-out civil war.

* * *

Alongside the dual power between the fascist-military government and the Republican (or "loyalist") side was *a dual power situation within the Republican forces*. The official state machinery had been rendered temporarily powerless while popular organizations fought the fascists and ran the economy. The central issue of the revolution was the relationship between the popular organizations and the Republican state.

On the Republican side there were two capitalist governments which mattered: the national government in Madrid and the regional government of Catalonia, centered in the city of Barcelona. This was the most industrialized region of Spain, with a working class and peasantry deeply influenced by anarchism. The Catalans, like their neighbors the Basques, had a tradition of struggling for cultural autonomy and perhaps national independence. The Republic had granted them a regional government with a certain degree of autonomy, the Generalidad. Both the Generalidad and the national Popular Front regime were left temporarily stranded, delicately balancing between the fascist-military rebellion--which had taken almost all its police-military forces--and the workers' and peasants' forces.

Having lost its army, the state had to rely on the workers' militias until it could rebuild a Republican capitalist army on authoritarian lines. The workers' parties and unions had created militias which marched on the fascists' positions and held the front against the them. These militias were more-or-less internally democratic, without differences in pay or condition between officers and the ranks, with election of officers, and with intense internal political discussion. There was a good deal of inefficiency and sloppiness about the improvised revolutionary army, but (as George Orwell argues) this was mostly due to its inexperience and thrown-together quality rather than to its egalitarian character. Over time, it became more efficient and self-disciplined, and would have become even more so had it not been stabbed in the back by the government and the union leaderships. Meanwhile, in the cities of the Republican zone, police tasks were carried out by committees of armed workers who patrolled the streets.

Faced with an economic strike and sabotage by the Spanish capitalists, the workers took over industry and ran it themselves (Dolgoff, 1974). In most factories and workshops throughout Spain , committees of employees were established. Wage rates were decided on by the workers. Coordination was organized through the unions. The telephones and the railroads, the gas and electricity, the barbershops and the textile industry, to mention a few examples, were reorganized by the workers. They were collectively run with efficiency. The workers started a munitions industry. After the defeat of the revolution, the returning capitalists sometimes noticed that their property had been maintained or even improved by the workers.

The Spanish revolution is the only revolution, to my knowledge, where the peasants voluntarily collectivized their land. Not only did they take over landed estates, but they turned them into cooperative, democratically self-managed farms instead of dividing them up into smaller plots. Where there were small farms, they were merged. Experiments were made in limiting or doing away with money. This was done in more than half the land in the Republican area, creating perhaps 1700 rural collectives (Dolgoff, 1974).

But, unlike the Russian revolution, these militia forces, worker street patrols, factory collectives, and peasant collectives were not coordinated by an overall structure such as the soviets. The peculiarity of the Spanish dual power was that the weak bourgeois government was counterbalanced only by a scattered set of popular organizations.

* * *

The Spanish revolution was faced with two--or perhaps two and a half--possible directions: reformism or consistent revolution--or centrism. The *reformist* argument had a seemingly commonsensical sound to foreign liberals. The important thing, according to this view, was to unite all "antifascist" forces. This required supporting the Republican government and holding off the revolution until after winning the war against Franco. Anything else would cause a war within the Republican side, a civil war within the civil war.

Furthermore it was essential to win support from the US, British, and French governments, for economic trade and to buy munitions. But they would only deal with the official Spanish government, not some revolutionary entity.

This was the policy of the "Popular Front," which had been advanced by much of the Spanish left well before the fascists revolted. That is, it was not just a temporary expedient in the extreme situation of the civil war but a long term strategy. It was unlike the "United Front" strategy, which advocated an alliance of the social democrats, Stalinists, anarchists, and any other working class organizations against the capitalists. Instead, the Popular Front approach proposed unity of the workers' organizations with the liberal wing of the capitalist parties. While both the United Front and the Popular Front policies advocated alliance and unity, one policy emphasized the class division (unity of the workers, peasants, and poor against the capitalists) and the other denied it (unity of the workers with the liberal wing of the capitalists). There is also an ambiguity in that the terms "people" or "popular" can be used to refer to the workers and all other oppressed sections (peasants, women, national minorities, etc.). However liberals and reformists use "the people" to refer to the oppressed together with the oppressors, workers and capitalists, that is, literally all the people.

The Popular Front was advocated by the Socialist Party, which led approximately half of organized labor through its UGT federation. These views were also supported by the Republican liberals, although they, of course, did not say they were for a revolution "after" the war. These were also the views articulated by the Spanish Communist Party. Upon the orders of the Russian Stalinist bureaucracy, the CP, in Spain and internationally, had just leapt from the ultra-left to the far right of the movement. They had been denouncing social democrats and other left tendencies as "social fascists," just as bad as fascists, refusing any United Front with the social democrats against the Nazis in Germany. Now they had become the strongest advocates of a Popular Front (the Russian state was trying to create an alliance with French and British imperialism against Germany). At the beginning of the civil war the

CP was quite small. It gained influence when the Russian government became the only foreign source willing to sell arms to the Spanish government. Part of the price for the armaments, besides the gold in Spanish banks, was inclusion of the CP in the Popular Front and placement of CPers in influential positions. Meanwhile the CP began to recruit widely from conservative middle class sectors.

Russian "advisors" were forced on the Spanish government, in return for arms sales while CPers were appointed to key places in the police and military. The CP built up its own apparatus, including secret police and private prisons which even the Spanish police could not control. It kidnapped, tortured, and killed political opponents on the left, such as Andres Nin of the POUM. It announced that it would treat Trotskyists and anarchists in Spain as it had in Russia.

As reasonable as the reformist case sounded to liberals abroad, it had several key weaknesses. One problem with the Popular Front strategy was that it was impossible for the Republicans to beat the regular army at its own game--since revolutionary war was ruled out. The fascists had the experienced, professional officers, a trained rank-and-file, a superior air force, and the original arms of the regular army plus a constant supply from Germany and Italy. The Republicans had to organize a regular army from scratch, and had limited arms. In a straight slugging match between two armies, the fascists would win--and did.

In the alternate strategy of *revolutionary war*, success would depend at least as much on psychology and politics as on ammunition. It was necessary to increase morale among the revolutionary armed forces and in the working population which supported it and to decease morale in the fascist ranks and to raise opposition to them in the enemy's rear. This would have been done, for example, by guaranteeing land to the peasants. Most of Spain was then a farming country; the ranks of the fascist forces were mostly peasants as was most of the population in their zone. A promise of land would have set a fire in the fascists' ranks. Instead, the Republican government did the opposite--attacking the peasant collectives by laws and by military force, breaking them up and asserting the rights of the landlords and rich.

Another weakness of the reformist strategy was that the British, French, and US governments had no intention of helping the Republicans (even though the French government was also a Popular Front regime led by the Socialist Leon Blum). They signed a "Non-Intervention Agreement", by which they agreed to allow no arms to be sent to either side in Spain, even though one "side" was the legal government. They were too worried that a loyalist victory would inspire workers' revolution. They also figured that the historic ties of British and French business to Spain would influence the fascists if they won. As it turned out, they were right; the Franco regime remained neutral in World War II. Nazi Germany and fascist Italy also promised nonintervention , but they poured military aid into the Franco army. The Spanish Socialists and Communists could have appealed to the French workers to put pressure on their government (which included the Socialist and Communist parties), but this would have required public criticism of the French Popular Front's capitulation to capitalism.

A revolutionary policy would also have offered national self-determination to the Arabs of Spanish Morocco. The fascist military bases were mostly in the Spanish colonies in north Africa. A large portion of the regular army's ranks was Arabs. It would have been a great blow against the fascist military to have promised self-determination (a choice of autonomy or independence) to the Arabs and to have sent nationalist agitators into Morocco. Moroccan nationalists offered to go and a few anarchists suggested such a policy. But this would have threatened the French and British imperialists control of *their* colonies in north Africa and the Middle East. The last thing the French and British capitalists wanted was the example of national freedom for an oppressed Arab colony. Because of its pro-Western-imperialist policy, the Spanish Popular Front government had tied its hands and could not use this weapon (assuming that the liberals had wanted an anti-colonialist policy in the first place).

Nor did the reformist strategy avoid the danger of a civil war within the Republican zone. Inevitably, the capitalist state had to rebuild itself and reassert its power. Even though the workers' and peasants' organizations did not challenge the state, the state had to challenge them. A situation of dual power must be resolved one way or another. Step by step the regime whittled away the powers of the popular committees. A regular army was built up and a police force created and armed. The radical militias were starved of weapons and ammunition and were gradually subordinated to the new regular army. Industrial self-management and socialization were undermined by either returning owners or by state supervision. Collectivized farms were broken up by force. Government censorship was imposed on the left press and political repression, including jailing and killing, increased. A flood of propaganda by the Communists denounced leftists as not merely wrong but as deliberate agents of fascism.

In May 1937, eleven months after the start of the fascist rebellion, this came to a climax with a government effort to seize the Barcelona telephone exchange from the anarchist workers. That set off a general strike and virtual uprising, with barricades being built and the workers' seizing control of most of Barcelona (an eyewitness account is given in George Orwell's *Homage to Catalonia;* 1980). This could have led to the workers' and peasants' taking power in Catalonia. Instead, the anarchist and leftist leaders persuaded the workers to go back to work in return for vague promises from the government. The result was a big defeat for the workers as the government turned to repression of the left, including the outlawry of the leftist POUM, jailing its leadership, even military officers.

While the reformist approach was strongly supported by the Communist Party and the right wing of the Socialist Party, unfortunately there was no major force advocating a revolutionary program. Instead, several forces advanced a *centrist* approach. Officially they favored a revolution but in practice they did not challenge the reformists. This was the policy of the left wing of the Socialists and also of the POUM (Workers Party of Marxist Unification). The POUM had been formed out of a merger of various oppositionist groups expelled by the Communist Party, including Trotskyists on the left and Bukharinists on the right. In Catalonia it was a large force. While smaller than the anarchists, it was larger than the Communists or even Socialists in the region. It had its own militia (in which Orwell served). Although presenting itself as the most revolutionary party, the POUM had supported the Popular Front and entered the capitalist government in Catalonia.

* * *

Unfortunately, centrism was also the policy of the Spanish anarchists. Unlike Russia or most other countries, the Spanish anarchists *had* organized themselves nationally. They did this after World War I to counter the threat of reformist trade unionists taking over the anarchist-syndicalist union federation (the CNT), on the one hand, and of Communists doing so, on the other (both of which had happened in France). They formed the FAI (Federation of Iberian Anarchists), a federation of small affinity groups, all of whose members had to belong to the CNT. They held regular congresses in which decisions were made. While not "democratic centralist," FAIists were loyal to the organization and to each other. Therefore they tended to carry out common positions and support the decisions of the organization in a self-disciplined manner. Spanish anarchists had long considered themselves a "vanguard," not in an elitist sense but as having "advanced" ideas, being "avant-garde." They did not speak of leaders but of "influential militants," which probably prevented them from democratically controlling the real leaders (see Bookchin, 1977). In any case, the most democratic structure in the world cannot make up for programmatic unclarity. Years of discussion had laid the basis for the rural collectives and workers' self-management of industry. But there had been little or no consideration of strategies for the situation in which they found themselves in 1936.

In July 1936, the workers of Catalonia had defeated the regional fascist rebellion. The CNT unions, led by the FAI, were in control of Barcelona and the region. Luis Companys, president of the Catalan Generalitat called the leaders of the CNT-FAI to his office. According to Garcia Oliver, a longtime anarchist militant and one of the participants, Companys admitted to them that the CNT-FAI was "the masters of the city." He offered to resign in their favor if they wanted but proposed instead that they work together. For the wily bourgeois politician this was only a first step to reestablishing the state and capitalism, as his later actions were to prove. But the anarchist labor leaders were naive and accepted his offer, eventually entering the Generalidad as ministers and then joining the central government (Garcia Oliver becoming Minister of Justice--an odd role indeed for an anarchist).

Garcia Oliver later claimed that the choice was "between Libertarian Communism, which meant an anarchist dictatorship, and democracy, which meant collaboration" (quoted in Richards, 1972, p. 35). As he saw it, if the CNT-FAI took power, it would have been a single-party dictatorship, "revolutionary totalitarianism." There is truth to this argument. Not all the workers in the CNT were actually anarchists, even if they followed the FAIists as union leaders. And there were other political tendencies within the working class and peasants as well as the middle class. Outside of Catalonia the CNT was somewhat smaller than the Socialist Party's UGT federation. What right did the anarchists have to force their policies on the whole of the working class, peasantry, and poor of Spain? Therefore the anarchist leadership saw no alternative to working with the reformists, the liberals, and the capitalist state: "democracy, which meant collaboration." In reality these arguments were rationalizations for capitulating to the pressures of the situation.

Obviously this denied everything the anarchists had taught about the authoritarian, undemocratic nature of the state and capitalism. Most anarchists were unhappy with these policies but did not know what to propose instead. They were loyal to the CNT and FAI and did not want to fight them. So they went about their business, fighting in the militia against the fascists, organizing factory committees, or working in rural collectives. (This seems to have been the situation of the great revolutionary anarchist Buenaventura Durriti; Paz, 1976). A few spoke out against anarchist participation in the government, but this was not enough to pose an alternate policy for the revolution. It was not enough for the anarchists to keep their hands clean. The military effort and the economy had to be coordinated somehow, by *someone.* If not by the existing state, than how and by whom?

There was, however, another alternative, which was both democratic and revolutionary. That was for *a federation of the factory committees, peasant collectives, workers' street patrols, militia councils. and other popular committees.* The CNT-FAI of Catalonia could have immediately called these to hold assemblies, have elections, and send delegates to a central council or federation of councils. Different political tendencies (anarchist, social democratic, Stalinist, bourgeois parties, etc.) would have been represented in proportion to their support in the working population, reflected by the number of delegates each got. Hopefully the most revolutionary elements and organizations would win popularity.

The anarchists could have immediately set up such federated popular councils in Barcelonia and the rest of Catalonia, and at least called for similar councils in the rest of Spain, using Catalonia as a revolutionary example. They could have been presented to the people as a democratic form of a United Front of the workers' organizations, an alternative to the then-powerless and abandoned capitalist state of the Republic.

A policy of workers' councils *had* been advocated even before 1936, by Trotsky and his handful of followers in Spain (Morrow, 1974; Trotsky, 1973; Guillamon, 1996). No doubt the Trotskyists saw the councils in an instrumental way, as a means for their party to take power (see Trotsky, 1961). But the point is that they had raised the council idea for Spain. Trotsky based this on the experience of the soviets in the Russian revolution, which had begun as councils for coordination of strikes and ended up taking power.

Near the end of the revolutionary period, a similar view was developed by an organization of Spanish anarchists, the Friends of

Durruti Group. This group was initiated by former members of the "Durruti" militia column who would not accept the state militarization policies, together with some revolutionary anarchist journalists, such as Jaime Balius. They denounced the collaborationist policies of the CNT-FAI leadership and called for a revolutionary program. In their 1938 programmatic statement, *Towards a Fresh Revolution,* they proposed "a slight variation in anarchism" (Friends of Durruti Group, 1978, p. 42). This was the "establishment of a revolutionary junta or national defense council." It would coordinate the militias and workers' patrols in waging the war, repressing fascists behind the lines, and handling international relations. Until this could be done, they were for cooperating with the existing system in a practical way, such as supporting the military struggle against the fascists and working in industry to produce armaments.

Unfortunately, the best book on the Friends of Durriti (Guillamon, 1996) misunderstands their position as similar to authoritarian socialism, equivalent to advocating a dictatorship of a minority vanguard party, or perhaps coalition of such parties. Guillamon writes, *approvingly*, "This Revolutionary Junta...others call...the vanguard or the revolutionary party" (p. 95). But their program did not call for a party-state. It explicitly declared that the defense council would be democratic: "Members of the revolutionary Junta will be elected by democratic vote in the union organizations." The unions would also work together with a federation of free municipalities.

This concept may be still too much tied to the traditional syndicalist idea of the primacy of the unions, as opposed to workplace and popular assemblies, but it is close enough to the council program in practice. Had they formed earlier, they might have been able to build a coalition with the left of the POUM, the few Trotskyists, and other anarchists, to fight for a program of revolutionary-democratic juntas. But by 1938 it was too late. The revolution had been politically defeated and it was just a matter of time until the fascist defeated the Republican armed forces on the battlefield .

* * *

Based on the Spanish experience, the Trotskyists made a criticism of anarchism. The anarchists failed to form a council system, and instead joined the capitalist government, they argued, due to a flaw in the anarchist theory. The anarchists were against all states, capitalist states as well as "workers' states," seeing them as essentially the same, all bad. Yet it became obvious in Spain that some social organ was needed to coordinate the struggle, repress the fascists, allow representation for different political groupings, and relate to foreign states. That is, the Trotskyists said, a state was needed. But since the anarchists did not see the need for a workers' state, they were willing to join the capitalist state, which was, they believed no better or worse than a workers' state.

There is, I think, some logic in this criticism. Anarchists *have* opposed or at least underemphasized *the need for power, for the oppressed to organize themselves to overthrow the oppressors and to suppress counterrevolutionary, fascist-like, forces*. Or at least anarchism is ambiguous about power. Anarchists often do not understand the need for the workers to take power, without creating a new state. For all the advantages the Spanish anarchists had, such as a national organization and years of discussions, they were woefully unprepared for a revolution. When a revolution came, they could see no alternative to either setting up a dictatorial party-state of the CNT-FAI or to joining the capitalist government.

On the other hand, the Trotskyist/Marxist argument only works if we accept the federation of workers' and people's councils as a state of some kind. This may seem like a quibble over words, but the Commune is different from any other kind of "state" in history. It is the self-organization of the big majority of the population rather than a minority organization over and above society. Its repressive functions are carried out against the formerly exploiting minority and it is consciously on the path to ending all repression. It is not, and cannot be, a "workers' state," because there is no such thing.

At the time, Trotsky and his followers were at their most libertarian. They were advocating overthrowing the Russian bureaucratic state and replacing it with a system of multiparty soviets/councils (Trotsky, 1977)--while *still* regarding the totalitarian Stalinist state as some sort of workers' state. Since then, the Trotskyists have pretty much dropped the council-state idea (Hobson & Tabor, 1988). Most orthodox Trotskyists have become uncritical supporters of the Cuban state (a one-party, one-man, dictatorship), supporters of the Russian invasion of Afghanistan, and denouncers of the collapse of the Stalinist state as a "counterrevolution." There are unorthodox Trotskyists, who correctly regard the Soviet Union as having been state capitalist rather than a "workers' state." Yet they too endorse the early Soviet Union of Lenin and Trotsky, when it was a one-party dictatorship.

Interestingly, Grandizo Munis, a leader of Spanish Trotskyism, may have been influenced to move in the direction of anarchism. He became a close friend of Jaime Balius, the theoretical leader of the Friends of Durruti, even living together for a while in exile in Mexico (Guillamon, 1996). This may have been a factor in Munis' eventual rejection of the Trotskyist "degenerated workers' state" theory of Russia in favor of a state-capitalist analysis and his rejection of the vanguard party approach (Hobson & Tabor, 1988). Munis was also a friend of Trotsky's widow, Natalia Sedova, who agreed with him, at least that Stalinist Russia was state capitalist.

Guillamon (1996), who seems to be a Bordigist (an authoritarian far-left tendency), sees the Friends of Durruti as essentially reinventing the wheel, recreating, in the "anarchist idiom," "old Marxist postulates" about the state, the need for a revolutionary program, and the need to organize for it (the "vanguard"). Even were this true, it would be significant that they did so within the anarchist tradition. In fact it is not true, since the concept of a federation of councils to coordinate a revolutionary war has long been part of anarchism. That the main anarchist organizations failed to live up to their program is a different matter.

While anarchism, as a movement, may have failed in Spain, Marxism cannot be said to have done very well either. Speaking of the Marxists as a whole, they capitulated to the liberal bourgeois state as badly (or worse) than the anarchists. The Socialists wallowed in statist reformism, and the centrist POUM, claiming to be revolutionary Marxist, talked about the need for a new state but actually joined the old one. The Stalinist CP was deliberately counterrevolutionary (which is not to deny the naive idealism of the ordinary members of these parties, even the Stalinists). The Trotskyists lost a section to the POUM centrists, were divided into two small groupings, and were never able to develop much popular influence. Only a small group of Marxists (the Trotskyists) and a small group of anarchists (the Friends of Durrutti and a few others) rejected participation in the bourgeois state in favor of an association of councils. *The working class paid dearly for the failure of its organizations to understand the need to replace the state with alternate institutions of popular power.*

But the practical effect of the defeat of the Spanish revolution was to wipe out the last chance of anarchism having significant international influence for generations. Due to its own weaknesses, as well as to objective factors, the Spanish anarchists suffered a defeat which set back the world movement and the hope for liberation. Anarchists had groupings in other countries but Spain was their last gasp in fighting fascism in the industrial centers of the world. Many militants throughout the world now concluded that the only hope for defeating Naziism and fascism in general was to support either Western or Russian imperialism or both. It was to be a long time for both Western democracy and Stalinism to be discredited enough at the same time, in order for libertarian socialism to reemerge as a viable force.

CHAPTER 11. THE FIGHT AGAINST NAZIISM IN GERMANY

To jump back in history, before the Spanish revolution, I will next discuss the counterrevolutionary victory of fascism--specifically Naziism--in Germany in 1933 (Gluckstein, 1999; Guerin, 1973; Trotsky, 1971). While the Spanish counterrevolution may be properly called fascist, because it smashed the working class organizations, it was mostly a military coup which turned into a civil war. Naziism was a "purer" form of fascism, a mass movement which took power, with the German military staying in the background. Again, the fight against fascism turned on the radicals' conceptions of the state.

In Germany in the thirties, the key question was the relationship between the bourgeois-democratic state (the Weimar republic) and the coming fascist state. The Communist Party, in its ultra-left phase claimed that they were the same (both varieties of fascism) and therefore there was no need to make a specific fight against Naziism. The Social Democratic Party seemed to think that they were utterly different, and therefore that the institutions of bourgeois democracy could be relied on to prevent fascism from taking power. Actually these are two different types of bourgeois state, opposed in that one was a (limited) democracy and one a dictatorship, but alike in being supporters of capitalism. The overthrow of bourgeois democracy was a "political revolution" and not a "social revolution." That is, the form of government was overthrown but the basic nature of the state and the capitalist system did not change. The capitalist class remained the upper class. This meant that it was necessary for the workers to defend their bourgeois democratic rights against Naziism, but a mistake to rely on the bourgeois democratic state to resist Naziism.

Today there has been a rise in political conservatism, a domination of the extreme right of the U.S. ruling class and the capitulation of the more moderate capitalist politicians. On a world scale their policies have been called "neo-liberalism." To say that this resembles the conditions under which fascism rose and triumphed over the left in the 1930s would be a gross exaggeration. And a real fascist threat in North America is unlikely to take the exact form as in Europe in the past. Yet issues are being raised now which resemble those raised in the struggle against Naziism and other forms of fascism. Many liberals fear that the U.S. is already under fascism or in danger of becoming fascist, due to the repressive, militarist policies of right-wing Republicans. This is a mistake. We are living under a bourgeois democracy, and this is what bourgeois democracy is, namely repressive and militarist. The U.S. still has elections (with a high level of fraud, of course), unions, free speech and organization for the Left (with various limitations), etc. None of this exists under fascism.

Exactly because we do not--yet--directly face a massive fascist threat makes this the right time to learn the lessons of the past, especially for anarchists and other libertarian socialists.

* * *

But first, a brief discussion of the fight against the rise of Fascism in Italy. In the 1920s in Italy, gangs composed of veterans of World War I began to be organized by right-wing forces. Benito Mussolini, a former left-wing socialist, organized them into the Fascist Party, and got subsidies from the rich. He used them to attack union headquarters and left-wing party meetngs.

Various anarchists called for a united front against the Fascist gangs (Rivista Anarchica,1989). The anarchists were a significant minority, leading their own syndicalist unions. They called for unity in action of the unions and left parties, to physically combat the fascists, to defend the workers' institutions, and to drive the fascists off the streets. To the extent they could, anarchists and anarchist-syndicalists carried this out, combatting the Fascists together with whomever would ally with them. In a number of cities they had some success in defeating the right-wing gangs for a time. But they were sabotaged by the left parties. The Socialist Party (Italian social democrats) was so craven that it actually disarmed itself by agreeing to a so-called Pact of Pacification with the Fascists in August 1921. The Italian Communist Party ordered its members not to work with the anarchists and denounced the idea of a united front. At that time, the CP was led by Amedeo Bordiga (later expelled from the Communist Internationa). His authoritarian sectarianism was a precursor of Third-Period Stalinism, discussed below. Without effective opposition, the Fascists took power in Italy, with the support of the king and the bourgeoisie. Feeling their way through a period when they maintained superficial democratic institutions, they eventually established a totalitarian state, with mass murder of the workers' forces. Italian fascism served as a model for Hitler.

* * *

Now, some background for Germany: World War I ended with Germany beating Russia and the Western Allies beating Germany. A revolutionary wave swept over Europe, although it has been dropped out of most history books. Only in the Russian Empire did revolutionaries come to power and stay there. In some parts of eastern Europe they took power briefly. In Italy the workers took over most of the north but were betrayed by the fearfulness of the Social Democratic Party.

The key country was Germany. In 1918 workers and soldiers successfully overthrew the old monarchist regime. The German cities, industries, and military bases were covered with councils organized by the workers and military rank and file (Harman, 2003). Once again the working class showed a tendency to replace the state by radically democratic councils (Raete in German). But the Social Democratic Party leaders made a deal with the army leadership to maintain the army, the state, and capitalism. Under the Social Democrats' orders, the revolution was drowned in blood, including the murder of Rosa Luxemburg. The unstable Weimar republic was established. In 1923, the fledgling Communist Party made another attempt at a German revolution, failing both because of inexperience and because of misdirection from Moscow (which was becoming Stalinized).

By the late twenties it was clear that a revolution was not about to happen but neither was the country stabilized. The single largest party was the Social Democratic Party, now in office and now out. Unlike today, Social Democrats then claimed to be socialists who were working for a new society. Their worker members believed them. Their bureaucratic leadership was committed to working within the system, believing in legality, parliamentarism, and peaceful business-union negotiations. To their left was the Communist Party, large but still smaller than the SDs. It included most of the revolutionary-minded workers. By this time, all independent thinkers, heirs of Luxemburg, had been driven out of the party. Its bureaucracy was completely subservient to Stalin's directions.

In the middle were various liberal or moderate capitalist parties, such as the Catholic Center Party. Over time they lost their base to the far-right. This was a medley of groupings, former military men, thugs out for excitement, and various crackpots. The largest became the National Socialist German Workers Party. Its name says something about its appeal, both National-German and Socialist-Workers. On the one hand it pumped up national pride, claiming that Germany had lost the war only because the socialists had stabbed the army in the back. On the other, it roused hostility toward the rich but channeled it against the Jews (leaving the Nazis free to sell themselves to the real rich).

After the crash of 1929 and the Great Depression, the National Socialists (or Nazis) grew rapidly. They drew from every class, but especially from the middle layers--ruined small businesspeople, professionals, shop-owners, white-collar workers, bureaucrats, lawyers, teachers, engineers, college graduates with no jobs, people who were furious at the rich but hated the poor, people who were anti-capitalist in some ways but feared falling into the proletariat. During periods of revolutionary upswing, many had turned to the working class parties. There had been unionization of white collar workers. But the Left had proven impotent to solve the social stalemate and now these people looked for someone with the power to do something--anything--to end the suffering. Adolph Hitler's program did not make much sense, being full of contradictory promises and superstitious ranting, but at least he promised action as well as feel-good rhetoric.

For Hitler, the key question was winning the support of the real centers of power, particularly the leading capitalists (also the generals). The fascists had begun by themselves. At first big business had not wanted the fascists. All things being equal, the capitalist class prefers a limited democracy. It lets them settle disputes among factions of their class without bloodshed. It lets them coopt oppositions, such as the Social Democrats or liberals. It fools the populace into thinking that they run the country. But things were getting out of hand during the Great Depression in Germany. Big business needed to smash the unions and the workers parties in order to lower their standard of living and raise profits. It needed to expand into eastern Europe and elsewhere for raw materials and other benefits (which fit the generals' desires also). They needed social order. So they became ready to hire the Nazis. At this point the Nazis were ready for power.

The Nazis offered the capitalists something more than just another authoritarian state, such as the monarchy or a bureaucratic police state. They had a mass movement, full of desperate middle class people, which could be used to really smash up the workers' parties and unions. They had organized thousands of uniformed thugs ready to fight the workers, break up their organizations, and drive down their standards of living. The Nazis did not just run in elections. They assaulted workers' meetings, beat up Social Democrats on the streets, stopped them from selling their papers, assassinated opponents, and generally created a reign of terror. The police would not control them. Judges let them off with slaps on the wrist. (The issue was not "free speech" for the Nazis but the failure of anyone to stop their murderous extralegal actions.)

To counter the growing fascist threat, the Social Democratic bureaucrats stuck to the old tried-and-true methods. They could not see that the National Socialists were not just another electoral party. The Social Democrats ran in elections and maneuvered in parliament. They kept up their organizations, their unions, their press, their workers' centers and clubs. They built a self-defense organization of militant workers, the Reichsbanner, which was held in reserve and almost never used in action. They did not see that Naziism could not be defeated by legalistic electoral methods.

Jumping ahead a bit, in 1932 there was the decisive election for the office of the president. Hitler ran. The Communist Party ran their leader. The conservatives ran an old monarchist general, von Hindenburg. The Social Democrats decided that it was essential to stop Hitler--and they believed this could be done through electoralism. They endorsed von Hindenburg, as the lesser (nonfascist) evil. Their slogan was "Smash Hitler, Elect Hindenburg!" Von Hindenburg was elected President. After some maneuvering, he appointed Hitler as Chancellor, which began the long night (Draper, 1972). Not that von Hindenburg was a Nazi; he thought these ruffians could be controlled by the respectable types--Hitler was *his* lesser evil. The Germans never gave the Nazis a majority of the vote, and yet they took power. We see that *even in this extreme situation, when the issue was life or death for the organized working class, electoralism did not work.* The struggle against fascism should have been done outside the framework of electoral tactics.

* * *

The key issue was the behavior of the Communist Party--a party with millions of revolutionary-minded workers shackled by its Stalinist bureaucracy. Unfortunately the party was completely disoriented by crazed directions from Moscow adopted at the end of the twenties and the beginning of the thirties. These directions said that the world had passed into an extremely revolutionary time, the so-called Third Period. The First Period had been the revolutionary upsurge after World War I, the Second had been a time of stabilization afterwards, in which reformist politics had been proper, and now was the Third Period. The struggle for reforms was to be abandoned. Communists were to leave the Social Democratic unions and form their own super-revolutionary unions (however small) and the final revolutionary battle was happening right now. This policy ignored the fact that most workers were still in the Social Democratic Party and its unions and that they had pulled back from revolution after the failures of the revolutionary attempts of 1918 and 1923. It ignored the immediate issue of protecting workers' democratic rights against fascism, not jumping into a revolutionary attempt.

Added to this approach was the theory of "Social Fascism." This said that not only were the fascists fascist, but so were all the other parties and tendencies except the Communist Party. This included the Social Democrats, who were "social fascists", another variety of fascism (anarchists were "anarcho-fascists"). Stalin declared to the world, "Fascism is the militant organization of the bourgeoisie which bases itself on the active support of the Social Democracy. Objectively, Social Democracy is the moderate wing of fascism...These organizations [fascists and Social Democrats] do not contradict but supplement one another. They are not antipodes but twins."

It is true that the reformists and liberals, including the Social Democrats, support capitalism. By their weaknesses they permit fascism to grow and to take power. But this is altogether different from saying that they are fascist! On the contrary, the Social Democrats had a stake in maintaining bourgeois democracy. Their electoral party, their unions, their other institutions, all depended on the existence of an elected government, freedom of speech, and freedom of association. The fascists on the other hand, would destroy elections as well as the workers' associations. (Even though this was before Hitler took power, there was the example of fascist Italy to make this clear.)

Since the Social Democrats were fascists, the Stalinists said, there could be no bloc with them against the Nazis, their fellow fascists. In fact, at one point the Communists even allied with the Nazis against the Social Democrats, supporting a referendum against a Social Democratic government in one region. Nor could there be any effort to defend democratic rights against the Nazis, on the grounds that bourgeois democracy was also fascist and no different from the rule of fascism. They ignored the fact that under bourgeois democracy the workers had their unions and parties while under real fascism these would be crushed, outlawed, and their leaders murdered--a big difference!. That is, the point should have been not to defend capitalist democracy but to defend the elements of workers democracy which it had been forced to let exist.

Since it seemed ridiculous to oppose any alliance with the Social Democrats, the CP called for a "United Front from Below." That is, they would ally with rank and file Social Democrats but not with the Social Democratic leaders. However, what made the Social Democratic workers Social Democrats was their support for their leaders rather than the Communist or other leaders or parties. They were not going to abandon their leadership and organizations in order to follow the Communist Party (except for those few who were prepared to quit the SDs and join the CP, which was not a United Front at all).

These positions (Third Period and Social Fascism) were not based on an objective analysis of the period, but on the needs of the Russian bureaucracy. It had begun rapid industrialization and rural collectivization. This frenetic drive resulted in millions dead of overwork and hunger, as well as a massive internal purge of former revolutionaries. The super-left program for the Communist Parties internationally was a reflection of Russian internal politics.

* * *

The Social Democrats were committed to legal, electoralist, tactics at all costs and the Communists were stuck with a crazed program. All other tendencies were small and marginal, including the anarchists. The

Trotskyists, for example, had only a few hundred followers. However, it is interesting to look at Trotsky's writings of the time, which raised an intelligent and realistic alternative orientation.

(It is controversial to claim that anarchists have something to learn from Trotsky. It is not uncommon for anarchists to say they have something in common with libertarian, humanistic, Marxists, but this is another matter. It is my belief that Trotsky [and Lenin] had different goals than anarchists do [their political goal being the rule of a centralized party over a centralized state running a centralized economy]--but their means overlap with those of anarchists. This is because [unlike the Stalinists, who are congealed, moribund, Leninists], Trotsky and Lenin really, really, wanted an international working class revolution. They tried very seriously to work out tactics and strategies for the working class to organize itself against capitalism and to overthrow it. Such tactics and strategies are often an area of weakness for anarchists. True, the Leninists' aim was to put their party in power. But they wanted to do this by a working class revolution--unlike the Stalinists, who have never organized working class revolutions. In brief, Trotsky's means overlap with those of libertarian socialists, while his programatic ends were different. A careful analysis of these means can produce useful ideas for anarchists, as in the struggle against Naziism. This does not at all imply agreement with the overall program of Trotskyism or even of Marxism.)

Trotsky directed his writing toward the Communists, for a good reason and a bad reason. The good reason was that the Communists included most of the revolutionary workers. The bad (or foolish) reason was that he still thought his people could get back into the Communist Parties of Germany and Russia. (Although he gave his life in fighting Stalinism, he never fully understood what it was nor how he had contributed to it.)

He warned the Communist workers that Naziism was not just another authoritarian movement. The notion that all existing bourgeois parties were fascist made it seem like the Nazis (the real fascists) were no different from them. Not that Naziism would replace capitalism (as some theorized later)--the big capitalists did quite well under the Nazis. But it was a mass movement. Once combined with the powers of the state, it would be uniquely repressive. It would utterly destroy the workers organizations. It would murder not just the workers' leaders but rank and file union members. It would have agents in every neighborhood and village, in every chess and sports club, on every shop floor. He warned,

"Worker-Communists, you are hundreds of thousands, millions, you cannot leave for any place; there are not enough passports for you. Should fascism come to power, it will ride over your skulls and spines like a tank. Your salvation lies in merciless struggle. And only a fighting unity with the Social Democratic workers can bring victory. Make haste, worker-Communists, you have very little time left" (Trotsky, 1971, p. 163)!

He proposed that the Communists offer an alliance to the Social Democrats, and expose the Social Democratic leaders if they refused it. This working class alliance (United Front) would have very practical goals. The parties (and their unions and other organizations) would agree to defend each other from Nazi attacks. In every city and every neighborhood they would set up joint defense committees. They would have mutual patrols to drive the Nazis from the streets. They would map out the fascist headquarters to carry the fight to them. They would form committees in shops and offices to check how business was supporting the fascists and to stop it. They would work out a common plan for a general strike in the event of the fascists taking power regionally or nationally.

All this was highly practical and concrete. It was Trotsky's hope that, under the conditions of fighting the Nazis, the defense committees and factory committees would act like the soviets (originally strike committees) of the Russian revolution--that the revolutionaries, at first in a minority, would come to predominate because they had the best program and the most militancy. Such committees could develop plans for a transition to socialism. As events progressed, they might serve as the basis for a revolution. *They might form the basis for replacing the capitalist state with a council system.*

Trotsky did not propose a merger of the Communists and Social Democrats. He did not want them to run joint candidates or to put out common literature (a "propaganda bloc"). This was an alliance, not a merger. "March separately, strike together!" he said. The workers would see the revolutionaries and the reformists in joint action, so they could compare them and chose the revolutionaries (as he saw the Communists). It was necessary (1) for the revolutionaries to separate themselves out from the reformists in order to have a clear program, to be able to raise their own revolutionary banner, and (2) to join in mass action, in the unions and mass movements, alongside of the reformists in order to persuade the majority of workers that the revolutionary program was the best.

These ideas may seem commonsensical to us, essentially what the Italian anarchists had advocated: a coalition of workers organizations for mutual defense against the fascists (stripped of Trotsky's ultimate goal of putting the Communist Party in power over the working class). Class against class. What was remarkable was the resistance to this raised by the Communist Party, committed as it was to its Social Fascist theory (if it could be called that). The CP leaders pointed out that the Social Democrats had betrayed the revolution in 1918, murdering many Communists, including Luxemburg, had been elected to positions in the capitalist government, including a regional police chief, taken responsibility for repressive acts, and so on. All of which was true, but none of which proved the Social Democrats were fascists. The SDs still relied on capitalist democracy while the Nazis would destroy capitalist democracy (not capitalism). Against the Nazis, said Trotsky, he would ally with "the devil and his grandmother," even with Social Democrats who had repressed revolutionaries. He wrote a fable, in the style of Aesop, "A cattle dealer once drove some bulls to the slaughterhouse. And the butcher came nigh with his sharp knife.

'Let us close ranks and jack up this executioner on our horns,' suggested one of the cattle.

'If you please, in what way is the butcher any worse than the dealer who drove us hither with his cudgel?' replied the bulls, who had received their political education in the institute of Manuilsky [Stalin's secretary of the Communist International].

'But we shall be able to attend to the dealer as well afterwards.'

'Nothing doing,' replied the bulls, firm in their principle, to the counselor. 'You are trying to shield our enemies from the left; you are a social butcher yourself.'

And they refused to close ranks" (Trotsky, 1971, p. 293).

* * *

The Nazis took power--more-or-less legally. They then abolished all elections and electoral parties, both the workers parties and the bourgeois parties. They outlawed the unions and arrested their leaders, as well as the leaders, and even ranks, of the workers parties, to the pleasure of their capitalist paymasters. To please these capitalists and the generals, they murdered those members of their own party who had actually believed in the left aspect of their rhetoric. They installed their people in every village, sports club, and factory. Eventually (Trotsky predicted) their middle class followers would be betrayed by the Nazis' continued support for big business. The Nazis would lose their need for a mass movement. Then the regime would devolve into another bureaucratic police state and lose its special militancy. But that was the future. Immediately the regime was strong enough to commit crimes unparalleled in the history of humanity (the Holocaust, among others). It took the might of U.S., British, and Russian imperialism to finally smash it.

The Communist and Social Democratic parties did nothing when the Nazis took power. There was no general strike, no rebellion. They were crushed with hardly a whimper. The Social Democrats voted for the Nazis' foreign policy statement in parliament, just before they were outlawed. Their unions offered to work with the Nazi government. This made it a massive defeat for the working class, whose effects reverberate to this day. Those SD leaders who were not captured and murdered, escaped to the West. They returned with the Allied armies to help establish another bourgeois democracy. The surviving CPers escaped to Russia. Many were killed by Stalin. Others came back with the Russian army, to establish their own totalitarian, state-capitalist, rule in East Germany.

The Communist Parties made no attempt to analyze their mistakes in program or theory. They continued to act as if everything they had done was correct. But they switched to the right. They swung past the United Front to the Popular Front. This meant a cross-class alliance, not only of the workers parties, but also with liberal capitalist parties. This was not just a temporary alliance on a specific issue. It was seen as a long-term alliance, aiming at joint political power. It meant that their program could not go past a pro-capitalist level, to maintain their alliance with the capitalist partner. But the capitalist party would always be a weak reed against fascism or other capitalist attack. Fascism does not threaten the capitalist class (their base) but does threaten the working class and its institutions. A Popular Front government came to power in France. We have seen the effects of the Popular Front in Spain, this time including even the anarchists.

Trotsky finally saw that the Communist Parties were hopeless and gave up on trying to rejoin them. He came to advocate a workers' revolution against the bureaucracy in the Soviet Union. He now advocated multiparty, multitendency, democratic soviets. But he still believed that Stalinist Russia was somehow a workers' state to be defended against capitalism, continuing to accept nationalized property as defining a workers' state. He tried to create a new, Fourth, International our of sheer willpower, which failed completely. The post-Trotsky Trotskyists became variants of social democrats or Stalinists or both.

PART III- CONCLUSION:
Revolutionary Democracy

CHAPTER 12: DEMOCRACY VERSUS THE STATE

The revolutionary and counterrevolutionary upheavals, such as have been described here, have repeatedly raised the possibility of replacing the bureaucratic-military state of capitalism with a stateless, self-managing, participatory, society. How shall this tendency be described? The language of Marxism, and state-socialism in general, has increasingly been discredited. There needs to be an alternate way of conceptualizing the program of direct, face-to-face, political and economic self-government. Many leftists have turned to another tradition, that of the democratic revolution. Democracy can be seen as a ground for opposition to the authoritarianisms of capitalist society (Laclau & Mouffe, 1985; Morrison, 1995; Mouffe, 1992, 1996; Trend, 1996; Wood, 1995). Socialism may be presented as part of the program for radical democracy, rather than the other way around.

"Democracy" has two contradictory class meanings today: the justification of the existing state versus a tradition of revolutionary popular liberation: democracy-from-above versus democracy-from-below. It is the ideological support of the existing "democratic" states of the West and elsewhere--precisely because democratic ideals are so attractive. Periodical elections and (relative) freedom of expression and association are used to justify a society where a few really rule over the majority. Capitalist democracy is used by competing factions of rulers to settle

their disputes relatively peacefully. It serves to coopt rebellious popular forces.

But democracy is also the cry of the oppressed against ruling elites--the idea that ordinary people should participate in, and control, the institutions which make up their society. It goes back to tribal councils, to classical Athens, to the great bourgeois revolutions of England, the U.S., and France, to the U.S. abolitionists, and, today, to ideals loved by millions. It is rights torn from rulers by the struggle and blood of the people. It is the standard for judging the state--and for condemning it.

For centuries the term "democracy" was a *radical* concept and a *class* concept (Wood 1998). To the ancient Greeks, it meant rule by the masses, by the poor, rather than by the rich aristocrats. Plato condemned it, because he favored aristocratic rule; Aristotle wanted a mixed government, with democratic elements counterbalanced by aristocratic ones (among which he included representation). For Rouseau and others, democracy meant *direct democracy*, face-to-face communal rule. As late as the U.S. revolution, most of the founding fathers regarded the concept of democracy with horror, as a synonym for "mob rule." They feared that the poor majority would vote to divide up the landed estates of the rich and would wipe out the debts which the poor owed the wealthy by voting for cheap money. They made all sorts of constitutional controls on the democratic aspects of the new society. Eventually, the widespread acceptance of the word "democracy" went hand-in-hand with a gutting of its radical, class, content.

This theoretical development is interesting to those who see *socialist-anarchism as nothing but the most extreme, consistent, and thoroughgoing democracy* (Price, 2000). Others, such as Paul Goodman (1965) and Noam Chomsky (1994), have claimed their versions of anarchism as extensions of the democratic tradition from Jefferson to John Dewey. Benjamin Tucker, the nineteenth century U.S. anarchist, said, "The anarchists are simply unterrified Jeffersonian democrats" (in Krimerman & Perry, 1966, p. 69). Emma Goldman's biographer says the great anarchist was "simply an extreme federalist-democrat"

(Drinnon, 1961, p. 132). George Barnard Shaw, in a work written to *attack* anarchism, concluded, "Anarchism means simply the utmost attainable thoroughness of democracy" (quoted in Drinnon, 1961, p. 132). The contemporary anarchist, Murray Bookchin (1995) writes, "...A free society will either be democratic or it will not be achieved at all" (p. 17).

Yet the historical relation between anarchism and democracy is highly ambiguous. This should not be surprising, considering how vague and open-ended have been both terms. The anarchist historian George Woodcock (1962) says that anarchism is "aristocratic," *not* democratic. The Marxist historian, Hal Draper (1990) attacks anarchism as antidemocratic (see below).

Nor are anarchists alone in rejecting democracy as relevant to a society without a state. In *State and Revolution*, Lenin writes, "The abolition of the state means also the abolition of democracy" because "democracy is a state" (1970, p. 346). There are obvious problems in saying, as Lenin did, that his goal was a society without democracy. However, I am focusing on the anarchists' relation to democracy because it has been discussed more.

In *What is Property?*, the first work to claim the term "anarchist," Proudhon explicitly counterposed it to "democrat:" "I hear some of my readers reply: ...'You are a democrat.' No... 'Then what are you?' I am an anarchist' " (quoted in Woodcock, 1962, p. 12). But years later, Proudhon advocated the replacement of the state by a democracy of voluntary producers' associations, "a vast federation of associations and groups united in the common bond of the democratic and social republic" (quoted in Guerin, 1970; p. 45).

Anarchism may offer a unique perspective on democracy's two meanings. Liberals and social democrats believe in democracy and may call themselves "democratic socialists." But while highly critical of aspects of the system, ultimately they succumb to the mystifying aspect of democratic theory. They accept the existing state as democratic, but hope to modify it, to make it "even more so." On the other hand, authoritarian revolutionaries--Stalinists, radical nationalists, etc.--do not fall for the democratic obfuscation of U.S. imperialism. But they intend to replace this state with a new state, one in which they are the new rulers. They reject popular self-management as an ideal.

Anarchists, however, can reject the claim that existing states should be supported because they are supposedly democratic, while continuing to hold up democracy as a liberating vision. But to do this, *anarchism and democracy must be accepted as compatible.* To clarify this issue, I will first discuss a criticism of anarchism from the standpoint of democracy, and then a criticism of democracy from the standpoint of anarchism.

*   *   *

Robert Dahl's *Democracy and Its Critics* (1989) is a major statement of the case for democracy, clearly written and thoughtful. Before plunging into his argument, he discusses two fundamental "objections" to democracy, namely anarchism and "guardianship." He defines anarchism, fairly enough, as, "a society consisting only of purely voluntary associations, a society without the state" (p. 37). He adds that these associations might well be managed as democracies. This makes clear that anarchism is not opposed to democracy but to the "democratic state." Unfortunately, he does not go on to explain what he means by "the state." He uses it, apparently, to mean "the major means of organized coercion" (p. 43, see also p. 359).

Dahl goes on to make an argument that some coercion is necessary and that anarchists are wrong to absolutely oppose all social coercion. The goal should be to "...minimize coercion and maximize consent" (p. 51). Essentially I agree with his goal. Whatever may be the case after generations of anarchist freedom, a newly-anarchist society will need some way to control individual psychopathic killers or violent organized counterrevolutionaries. However, Dahl admits that preliterate peoples, such as the Inuit (Eskimo), lived satisfactorily for millennia without states, but he does not consider how they dealt with the social need for coercion (for the anarchist view, see Barclay 1990).

As I have noted, anarchists, like Marxists, have defined the state as an political-military institution arising out of and dominating the rest of society through special organs of coercion: the police, prisons, the military, and a political bureaucracy. The argument of anarchists is that it is possible to abolish the bureaucratic, socially-alienated institution of the state. The "democratic state" is to be condemned, not because it is still coercive, but because it cannot be truly democratic. By its very nature, this instrument of coercion which stands above and against society must serve a ruling minority against an oppressed majority.

Dahl does not deal with this issue directly, but it relates to a major point of his book. Modern society, he says, is too large and complex to be based on the face-to-face, direct democracy of the preliterate tribes or later city-states. For democracy to exist on a large scale, it needed the "invention" of representation. Only representative government (by implication, a state) could have brought democracy to the modern world, he claims.

But this has two sides. Representation made a sort-of-democracy possible on the large scale of modern nations, but that large scale made it possible to create a form of elite rule which could still be called democracy. Instead of direct, participatory democracy, we have a layer of elected politicians and government bureaucrats who stand between the people and the actual making of decisions. From time to time, the passive citizens elect these "representatives" to be political *for them*. As Wood (1995) points out, the US Founding Fathers argued that it was a virtue of a large republic that it required representation, which would act as a filter for the passions of the masses.

Undoubtedly, some degree of representation or delegation, from lower to higher bodies, is necessary. As federalists, anarchists have generally agreed with this. The meaning of "representation," and all other aspects of democracy, would change drastically in a different social context. The anarchists' proposed changes in society might be summarized in two concepts:

First is the creation of an egalitarian society in which separate groups of oppressor and oppressed either do not exist any longer (capitalists and workers) or have redefined their relationships as equals (men and women, European-Americans and African-Americans, North

Americans and Latin Americans). Where wealth is evenly distributed and no oppression exists, society is no longer pulled in different directions by competing and hostile forces. It does not need a state to hold things together; it is easier to maximize consent and minimize coercion.

Second, anarchists want a society based on direct democracy through popular assemblies--at the workplace, in the community, and in many voluntary associations. The more decisions are made locally, then the fewer are made centrally. The more people experience face-to-face democracy as a vibrant, daily, way of life, the more they will really control any representatives sent to delegated assemblies. "If the entire people were truly sovereign, there would no longer be either government or governed...the State...would be identical to society and disappear into industrial organization" (Guerin, 1970; p. 17).

Dahl is aware of these arguments and agrees with them to a point. He seeks to decrease social and political inequalities. He advocates greatly increasing participation and decision-making at the local community level. He supports a democratic socialism where the economy is socially owned and regulated but firms compete with each other. Unlike most supporters of "market socialism," he advocates that the firms be democratically managed by their employees, like producer cooperatives or the previous Yugoslavian system. "...It would be a mistake to underestimate the importance of authoritarian institutions in the daily lives of working people and the consequences of introducing a more democratic system in the governing of economic enterprises" (p. 332).

Yet he dismisses the idea of a drastic transformation of society raised by either Marxists or anarchists. "Market socialism" itself suggests that, even under "socialism," the economy will not be run overall by democratic decision-making but by the market. While agreeing that our society is highly unequal, he denies that there is minority rule (because there are competing elites). This society--which he calls "polyarchy"--is imperfect, but he argues that it is still democratic and worthy of support.

In effect, he acceptis the role of democracy as justifying the existing capitalist state.

Part of the problem is that, whenever he backs up theory by referring to practice, Dahl always turns to existing democratic bourgeois states. Using these as models produces a rather limited view of what democracy is capable of being. Anarchists focus on the historical revolutions (Bookchin, 1996; Dolgoff, 1974; Kropotkin, 1986; Voline, 1974)--as I have done in the last section.

Murray Bookchin (1996) reviewed revolutions from the 16th century peasant uprisings during the Reformation to the rebellions of modern industrial workers and peasants. He found that they repeatedly replaced states by communal self-organization. The oppressed people repeatedly created face-to-face directly democratic assemblies and/or elected councils of deputies, recallable, with limited mandates.

Summarizing the lessons of the 1956 Hungarian revolution, Anderson wrote, "For years to come all important questions for revolutionaries will boil down to simple queries: Are you for or against the program of the Hungarian revolution? Are you for or against workers' management of production? Are you for or against the rule of the Workers' Councils?" (1964, p. 7).

* * *

The relation of antistatism and democracy has been raised from the other side, by Errico Malatesta, the great Italian anarchist (active from the 1870s to the 1930s). Unlike the individualist, anti-organizational tendency within anarchism, Malatesta advocated that anarchists organize themselves and promote the self-organization of working people. In the 1920s, he wrote two brief pieces on our topic, with the theme summarized in the title of one, "Neither Democrats nor Dictators: Anarchists" (Malatesta, 1995; pp. 73-76 and 76-79).

He believed that the capitalist democratic state was preferable to a dictatorship, if only because anarchists could use its ideology against it. "...The worst of democracies is always preferable, if only from the educational point of view, than [Note] the best of dictatorships...

Democracy is a lie, it...is, in reality, oligarchy, that is, government by the few to the advantage of a privileged class. But we can still fight it in the name of freedom and equality..." (p. 77).

As can be seen from this, much of his opposition to democracy is really directed against democratic ideology as a rationalization for capitalism and the state. But he mixes this up with a denunciation of the very concept of majority rule. "...We are neither for a majority nor for a minority government; neither for democracy nor for dictatorship.... We are...for free agreement....We are for anarchy" (p. 76).

The democratic concept is "the rule of the majority, with respect for the rights of the minority." Under capitalism, these terms have been used to justify exploitation and oppression. "Majority rule" has meant the rule of the dominant minority which shapes majority public opinion through the control of media and in other ways. "Minority rights" has often been called on against any attempt by the majority to take any of the wealth of the rich. But "majority rule" and "minority rights" have also been rallying cries against ruling minorities and the prejudiced mass which follows them.

Malatesta points out that the majority is often wrong, compared to the most enlightened minority. If the majority rules, he argues, it must dictate to the minority, forcing its will on the minority. This is just as bad as minority rule, he claims. How can the majority be trusted to respect minority rights if the majority rules over the minority? For these reasons, Malatesta rejects majority rule in principle. Such views must be responded to.

Civil libertarians have long argued that there are many areas of life where collective decision-making is not necessary. In these areas, such as sexual orientation, the majority has no right to dictate to the minority. Large numbers of people today would respect the rights of "consenting adults" to engage in minority sexual practices. Thomas Jefferson argued for religious freedom, "...It does me no injury for my neighbor to say there are twenty gods or no God. It neither picks my pocket nor breaks my leg" (Jefferson, 1957; p. 111). Anarchists seek to vastly expand the range of voluntary association for such self-chosen activities, activities outside the realm of majority rule.

However, there will still be areas which require collective decision-making. For example, a community may need to decide whether to build a new road. Consensus would be best, but people often disagree. A majority and a minority may polarize about this issue. This cannot be treated as a matter of voluntary association (although dissidents are always free to pick up and go elsewhere--but other communities also must decide whether to build roads). Either the road is built or it is not. If a majority forms for road-building, then the anti-builder minority may be asked to participate, to give their share of the labor or social wealth. In any case, they will have to live in the community with a new road, unwanted by them.

This is not coercion by the police but by reality. A decision had to be made collectively. If not determined by majority vote, then how? A community may decide that such decisions must be unanimous. But what if everyone cannot agree? Perhaps the minority gets to veto the proposal, since it is not unanimous. Then it is the minority which rules, preventing the majority from getting its road. Alternately, the minority agrees to keep quiet, so as to "not block consensus." This denies them the right to be openly counted as disagreeing. I do not deny the right of any community or association to decide to rely on consensus, but I am arguing that majority rule is not authoritarian in principle.

Malatesta asks what rights the minority has under majority rule. People with minority views have the right to participate in all decision making. They have the right to try to win a majority to their views. If they lose one vote, they may continue to participate and to seek to become the new majority. Perhaps in the future they will persuade enough community members that the new road was a mistake and to tear it down, or, at least, not to build new ones. They may be in the majority on other issues.

Minority rights is an essential part of majority rule. If the members of a community do not have the chance to hear all opinions, including minority ones, then they cannot be said to really decide the issues. The suppression of minority views in capitalist democracy (by force or just by lack of money or lack of coverage in the media) is one way the ruling minority creates the illusion that the majority is governing.

At the same time, minority rights are safest when the majority rules, democracy, as opposed to any minority dictatorship. *Majority rule and minority rights are not opposites but require each other.*

To democracy, Malatesta counterposes "free agreement." But there is no such opposition. People may freely agree to form voluntary associations--whether to trade stamps or to produce shoes. But then how will they run the associations? Presumably people will not agree completely on everything. There must be some process other than dissolving the associations each time everyone fails to agree. That process is democracy. Anarchists are not for a democratic state but can be for a democratic society. *Anarchism is democracy without the state.*

There may be tendencies toward hierarchy in a nonstate democracy. But it is mistake to use an absolutist yardstick in measuring all social programs, namely whether there are any elements of hierarchy, or any danger of hierarchy, in the proposal. If there are, then some purists will reject the program, however otherwise attractive. I propose instead the standard that the proposal be as decentralized and nonhierarchical as is likely to be workable, and only as centralized and hierarchical as is minimally necessary. I assume that some centralization is necessary, expecting that it will decrease over time as people work at it (at *withering it away*). The question is how to make society as participatory as we can.

There will be conflicts in a society without a state. Anarchism does not solve all human disagreements. No doubt the majorities in some councils will throw their weight around, ignoring the interests of the minorities. The minorities will have to organize to fight for their rights, seeking to persuade enough of the majority to come over to their side, and perhaps using other measures (strikes, civil disobedience). In other councils, minorities may dominate, such as cliques of good talkers and influential family members. The majority will have to organize to open things up for greater democracy. Elected bodies may come to dominate. There will have to be campaigns to elect people who will oppose the dominating policies of the elected committees. In short, anarchist-communism will not be a perfectly harmonious society, created by some formula for nonhierachy. It will live by the saying, "Eternal vigilance is the price of liberty." It will be full of lively debate and organizing, which is what is meant by democracy as a way of life.

* * *

Why is this important? We can see what happens when radicals try to develop democratic theory without incorporating anarchism. Often it is little more than "democratic socialism" restated, that is, reformist state socialism. For example, Trend's *Radical Democracy* (1996) is mostly articles by members of the reformist Democratic Socialists of America. They are somewhat embarrassed by the identification of their socialism with statism, but they still have no alternative to using the existing state to intervene in the economy.

A democratic theory which is really radical would strongly *deny that the existing capitalist state is truly democratic, would oppose the whole socially-alienated, bureaucratic-military state machine, and would propose instead a democratic federation of assemblies and associations.* Anything less will gloss over the antidemocratic nature of our society and its state.

A significant attempt to develop a radical democratic theory which includes socialism has been made by Chantal Mouffe and those associated with her. She is quite clear that *her "radical democracy" is not an alternative to the existing state but an extension of it.* "What we advocate is a kind of 'radical liberal democracy'--we do not present it as a rejection of the liberal democratic regime or the institution of a new political form of society" (1996, p. 20).

In fact the only time she seems to directly deal with the state is in a discussion of those who oppose "civil society" to "the state" (in Laclau & Mouffe, 1985). It is not hard to show that "civil society"--the realm of capitalism, patriarchy, and racism--is not the ground for salvation from the state. "Civil society" is internally antagonistic, based on the tensions between oppressed and oppressors.

Mouffe claims that the state also has internal antagonisms, therefore implying that it is wrong to reject the state as such. She notes, for example, that the state may pass legislation against gender discrimination or in defense of peasants against landlords in poor countries. This is true, but, to repeat, these are like raises which the management of a business may offer its workers. It may do this because the workers force it to or because it is far-sighted and provides benefits before the workers form a union--but whatever the reason, management remains capitalist and the enemy of the workers. There are divisions within management, as within the state, but they are over how best to suppress and/or coopt the oppressed. Neither management nor the state is the friend of workers or women or peasants. They must be pressured from the outside, not joined.

Laclau and Mouffe add that there are times when the state is opposed to "civil society," There are oppressive regimes where the state is " a bureaucratic excrescence imposed by force upon the rest of society." (p. 180) That is, in countries, such as the US, where the majority do support the regime, the state is not, they claim, a bureaucratic-military excrescence upon society. This is an opinion held by many people, including that US majority. It can be argued for, but I do not see how it can be called "radical."

* * *

If democratic theory needs anarchism, so *anarchism needs democracy*. There is an authoritarian trend within the history of anarchism, as I have argued. Anarchists have often been attracted to either reformism (support of the current state) or to support for revolutionary Stalinist states. Goodman (1994) and Chomsky (1987) could fairly be called reformists. Bookchin's electoralism has been discussed. This was a serious matter when the Spanish anarchists of the 1930s, faced with a revolutionary situation, became ministers in the liberal capitalist government. On the other side, many anarchists joined with the

Bolsheviks after the Russian Revolution. In the 1960s, the anarchist-pacifists of *Liberation* magazine became apologists for Castro and Ho Chi Minh. Further examples are easily found.

The Marxist historian Hal Draper (1969, 1990, 1992) has argued that the basic problem with anarchism is its supposed rejection of democracy. The essence of anarchism, he says, is a belief in the supremacy of the individual, the right of individuals to do as they want, without control from a ruling minority or even a democratic majority. Anarchism, he says, rejects any notion of democratic-control-from-below of society, even the most perfect, socialist-democratic, control, because it admits no limits on the individual. He quotes Proudhon, "Any man who cannot do what he wants and anything he wants has the right to revolt, even alone, against the government, even if the government were everybody else" (1992, p.12). He comments, "The only man who can enjoy this 'freedom' unlimited by society is a despot" (same). Draper cites evidence of anarchist authoritarianism in Proudhon's private notebooks where he plans to set up his mutualist association with himself as dictator, or Bakunin's fantasies of secret, super-centralized, "brotherhoods," which would control mass movements from behind the scenes.

While there is an authoritarian side of the anarchist tradition, it would be ridiculous to deny that there is also a libertarian-democratic side, in both theory and practice. Whether or not they used the word "democracy," socialist-anarchists have long advocated replacing bureaucratic institutions by self-governing associations, that is, by democracy (and, as I have argued, a strong defense of individual and minority rights does not necessarily contradict democracy or even majority rule). Anarchists have organized mass democratic labor unions, popular armies, and self-managed peasant collectives and worker cooperatives. Marxism too has both democratic and authoritarian sides, but the dominant tendency of its main wings, social democracy and Stalinism, has been authoritarian statism. Between Marxism and anarchism, it is anarchism which has the more democratic and freedom-loving theory and tradition. Also, anarchists have a different relation to their theoreticians than does Marxism and Leninism. We are "anarchists," not "Proudhonists" or "Bakuninists." Anarchism is not tied to its historic figures and has no problem rejecting their errors.

However, anarchism, if not inherently hostile to democracy, has had a contradictory relationship with it. The individualist tendencies are the worst in that regard, in effect, recreating the justification for aristocracy. What is needed is for anarchists to identify anarchism as extreme, revolutionary democracy. The weaknesses of anarchism are real, but they can be corrected from within the anarchist tradition

The program of anarchism is to replace the bureaucratic-military state machine with a federation of popular assemblies and associations, as decentralized as is practically possible. This is democracy without the state. Any other program, such as staying within the limits of the existing state but making it "more democratic" ("democratic socialism" or "radical-liberal democracy") capitulates to "democracy" as an ideological cover of the rule of a minority--of patriarchal-racist capitalism and its bureaucratic state.

REFERENCES

Albert, Michael, & Hahnel, Robin (1981). *Socialism today and tomorrow.* Boston: South End Press.

Albert, Michael, & Hahnel, Robin (1991). *Looking forward; Participatory economics for the twenty-first century.* Boston: South End Press.

Allen, Theodore W. (1994). *The invention of the white race (vol. 1): Racial oppression and social control.* New York: Verso Books

Alternate Defence Commission (1983). *Defence without the bomb.* London, UK: Taylor & Francis.

Anderson, Andy (1964). *Hungary '56.* London: Phoenix Press.

Avakian, Bob (1997). *MLM vs. anarchism.* Chicago: Revolutionary Worker.

Avrich, Paul (1970). *Kronstadt 1921.* New York: W.W. Norton.

Avrich, Paul (1973) (Editor). *The anarchists in the Russian revolution.* Ithaca, NY: Cornell Paperbacks/Cornell University Press.

Avrich, Paul (1995) (Editor). *Anarchist voices; An oral history of anarchism in America.* Princeton, NJ: Princeton University Press.

Bakunin, Michael (1980). *Bakunin on Anarchism.* (Sam Dolgoff, Ed.). Montreal: Black Rose Books.

Barber, Benjamin R. (2003). *Strong democracy; Participatory politics for a new age (20th aniversary edition).* Berkeley: University of California.

Barclay, Harold (1990). *People without government; An anthropology of anarchy.* London: Kahn & Averill.

Barnaby, Frank, & Boeker, Egbert (1982). *Defence without offence; Non-nuclear defense for Europe.* London, UK: Housmans.

Biehl, Janet with Murray Bookchin (1998). *The politics of social ecology; Libertarian municipalism.* Montreal: Black Rose Books.

Bookchin, Murray (1978). *The Spanish anarchists: The heroic years 1868--1936.* New York: Harper & Row/Colophon Books.

Bookchin, Murray (1980). *Toward an ecological society.* Buffalo, NY: Black Rose Books.

Bookchin, Murray (1986a). *The limits of the city* (2nd rev. ed.). Buffalo, NY: Black Rose Books.

Bookchin, Murray (1986b). *Post-scarcity anarchism* (2nd ed.). Buffalo, NY: Black Rose Books.

Bookchin, Murray (1995). *Social anarchism or lifestyle anarchism; An unbridgeable chasm.* Edinburgh, Scotland: AK Press.

Bookchin, Murray (1996). *The third revolution; Popular movements in the revolutionary era.* (Vol. 1). London, UK: Cassell.

Borsodi, Ralph (1972). *Flight from the city; An experiment in civilized living on the land.* New York: Haper Colophon Books.

Bradford, George [Watson, David], 1989. *How deep is Deep Ecology? With an essay-review on women's freedom.* Ojai CA: Times Change Press.

Brenan, Gerald (1971). *The Spanish labyrinth: An account of the social and political background of the civil war.* London: Cambridge University Press.

Brenkman, John (1987). *Culture and domination.* Ithaca and London: Cornell University Press.

Buber, Martin (1958). *Paths in utopia* (Trans. R.F.C. Hull). Boston: Beacon Press.

Bukharin, Nikolai (1981). Anarchy and scientific communism. In *The poverty of statism; Anarchism versus Marxism: A debate* (Albert Meltzer, Ed.). (pp. 1--10). Minneapolis, MN: Soil of Liberty.

Burnheim, John (1989). *Is democracy possible? The alternative to electoral politics.* Berkeley/Los Angeles: University of California Press.

Cannon, James A. (1962). The IWW; The great anticipation. In *The first ten years of American Communism* (pp. 277--310). New York: Pathfinder Press.

Castoriadis, Cornelius (1984). *Workers' councils and the economics of a self-managed society.* Philadelphia: Wooden Shoe Books.

Castoriadis, Cornelius (1997). *The Castoriadis reader* (David Ames Curtis, Ed. and Trans.). Malden, MA: Blackwell Publishers.

Chomsky, Noam (1993). *Year 501; The conquest continues.* Boston: South End Press.

Chomsky, Noam (1994). *Keeping the rabble in line; Interviews with David Barsamian.* Monroe, ME: Common Courage Press.

Class War Federation (1992). *Unfinishd business...; The politics of the Class War Federation.* London, UK: A.K. Press.

Cole, G.D.H. (1980). *Guild socialism restated.* New Brunswick, NJ: Transaction.

Commoner, Barry (1974). *The closing circle; Nature, man, and technology.* NY: Bantom Books/Knopf.

Dahl, Robert (1985). *A preface to economic democracy.* Berkeley/Los Angeles: University of California Press.

Dahl, Robert (1989). *Democracy and its critics.* New Haven: Yale University Press.

Davis, John (1978). *Technology for a changing world.* London: Intermediate Technology Publications..

Declaration of Independence (1996). Bedford MA: Applewood Books.

Deutscher, Isaac (1954). *The prophet armed; Trotsky: 1879-1921; vol. 1.* New York: Vintage Books/Random House.

Dickson, David (1974). *The politics of alternate technology.* NY: Universe Books.

Dolgoff, Sam (ed.) (1974). *The anarchist collectives; Workers' self-management in the Spanish revolution 1936-1939.* NY: Free Life Editions.

Draper, Hal (1969). A note on the father of anarchism. *New Politics.* Vol. VIII, no. 1. Pp. 79-93.

Draper, Hal (1972). Who is going to be the lesser evil in '68? In Michael Friedman (Ed.). *The new left of the sixties* (pp. 55-61). Berkeley, CA: Independent Socialist Press.

Draper, Hal (1987). *The "dictatorship of the proletariat" from Marx to Lenin.* New York, Monthly Review Press.

Draper, Hal (1990). *Karl Marx's theory of revolution; Volume IV: Critique of other socialisms.* New York: Monthly Review Press.

Draper, Hal (1992). The two souls of socialism. In E. Haberkern (ed.) *Socialism from Below.* NJ: Humanities Press. Pp. 2-33. www.ana.edu.au/polsci/Marx/contemp/pamsetc/twosouls (Site maintained by Rick Kuhn, School of Social Sciences, Faculty of Arts and Sciences, Australian National University)

Draper, Hal (1998). *The adventures of the Communist Manifesto.* Berkeley, CA: Center for Socialist History.

Drinnon, Richard (1961). *Rebel in paradise; A biography of Emma Goldman.* New York: Beacon Press/Bantam Books.

Drucker, Peter (1999). *Max Shachtman and his left; A socialist's odyssey through the "American Century."* Amherst, NY: Humanity Books.

Ehrenberg, John (1992). *The dictatorship of the proletariat; Marxism's theory of socialist democracy.* NY: Routledge.

Engels, Frederick (1954). *Anti-Duhring: Herr Eurgen Duhring's revolution in science.* Moscow: Foreign Languages Publishing House.

Engels, Frederick (1972a). On authority. In Karl Marx, Frederick
    Engels, & V.I. Lenin. *Anarchism and anarcho-syndicalism*. New
    York: International Publishers.

Engels, Frederick (1972b). *The origins of the famiiy, private property,
    and the state.* (E. Leacock, ed.). NY: International Publishers.

Fabbri, Luigi (1981). Anarchy and "scientific" communism. In *The
    poverty of statism; Anarchism versus Marxism: A debate* (Albert
    Meltzer, Ed.). (pp. 11--49). Minneapolis, MN: Soil of Liberty.

Farber, Samuel (1990). *Before Stalinism: The rise and fall of soviet
    democracy.* London: Verso.

Fernbach, David (1974). Introduction. *Karl Marx: The First
    Internatonal and after; Political writings, Vol III.* (pp. 9--72). New
    York; Vintage Books/Random House.

Finley, M.I. (1985). *Democracy, ancient and modern (rev. ed.).* New
    Brunswick, NJ: Rutgers University Press.

Fotopoulos, Takis (1997). *Towards an inclusive democracy.* London:
    Cassell.

Friends of Durriti Group, The (1978). *Towards a fresh revolution*
    (trans. Paul Sharkey). Sanday, Orkney, UK: Cienfuegos Press,
    Over the Water, New Anarchist Library.

Fromm, Erich (1955). *The sane society.* New York: Holt Rinehart and
    Winston.

Futrelle, David (1994, November/December). Is there life beyond
    the Democrats? *Utne Reader*, no. 66 (pp. 17--19).

Gluckstein, Donny (1999). *The Nazis, capitalism, and the working
    class.* London/Chicago: Bookmarks.

Goodman, Paul (1960). *Growing up absurd; Problems of youth in the
    organized society.* New York: Random House.

Goodman, Paul (1962). *The society I live in is mine.* New York:
    Horizon Press.

Goodman, Paul (1965). *People or personnel; Decentralizing and the mixed system*. NY: Random House.

Goodman, Paul (1994). *Decentralizing power: Paul Goodman's social criticism* (ed. Taylor Stoehr). New York: Black Rose Books.

Goodman, Paul, & Goodman, Percival (1960). *Communitas; Means of livelihood and ways of life*. New York: Vintage Books/Random House.

Grenier, Guillermo J. (1988). *Inhuman relations: Quality circles and anti-unionism in American industry*. Philadephia: Temple University Press.

Guerin, Daniel (1970). *Anarchism; From theory to practice*. (M. Klopper, trans.) NY: Monthly Review Press.

Guerin, Daniel (1973). *Fascism and big business*. NY: Pathfinder.

Guerin, Daniel (1998). *No gods, no masters; Book two* (trans. Paul Sharkey). San Francisco: AK Press.

Guillamon, Agustin (1996). *The Friends of Durruti group: 1937--1939* (trans. Paul Sharkey). San Francisco: AK Press.

Haberkern, E. (1992). Introduction. *Socialism from Below*. NJ: Humanities Press. Pp. xv--xviii.

Harman, Chris (2003). *The lost revolution: Germany 1918 to 1923*. Chicago: Haymarket.

Harrington, Michael (1964, Summer). Should the left support Johnson? Yes. *New Politics, iii*, 3. Pp. 6--10.

Harrison, Frank (1983). *The modern state; The anarchist analysis*. Montreal: Black Rose Press.

Hart, Gary (1998). *The minuteman: Restoring an army of the people*. New York: Free Press.

Hess, Karl (1979). *Community technology*. New York: Harper & Row.

Hobson, Christopher Z., & Tabor, Ronald D. (1988). *Trotskyism and the dilemma of socialism*. New York: Greenwood Press.

Hook, Sidney (2002). *Towards the understanding of Karl Marx; A revolutionary interpretation.* Expanded edition. (Ernest B. Hook, editor). Amherst, NY: Prometheus Books.

Horowitz, Irving Louis (Ed.) (1964). *The anarchists.* New York: Dell Publlishing.

International Revolutionary Solidarity Movement/First of May Group (1980). *Towards a citizens' militia; Anarchist alternatives to NATO and the Warsaw Pact.* Over-the-Water, Sandy, Orkney, UK: Cienfuegos Press.

Jefferson, Thomas (1957). *The living thoughts of Thomas Jefferson; Presented by John Dewey* (John Dewey, Ed.). Greenwich, CT: Fawcett Publications.

Jenkins, David (1974). *Job power: Blue and white collar democracy.* New York: Penguin Books.

Johnson, Ana G. & Whyte, William F. (1982) The Mondragon system of worker production cooperatives. In Lindenfeld, Frank, & Rothschild-Whitt, Joyce (Eds.). *Workplace democracy and social change* (pp. 177-197). Boston: Porter Sargent Publishers.

Kellerman, Jonathan (1999). *Savage spawn: Reflections on violent children.* NY: Library of Contemporary Thought/Ballantine.

King-Hall, Stephen (1960). *Common sense in defence.* London, UK: K-H Services.

Kotz, David, & Weir, Fred (1997). *Revolution from above: The demise of the Soviet system.* New York: Routledge.

Krimerman, Leonard I., & Perry, Lewis (Eds.) (1966). *Patterns of anarchy; A collection of writings on the anarchist tradition.* Garden City, NY: Anchor Books/Doubleday.

Kropotkin, Peter (1975). *The essential Kropotkin* (Emile Capouya & Keitha Tompkins, Eds.). New York: Liveright.

Kropotkin, Peter (1986). *The geat French revolution; 1789-1793.* (N. F. Dryhurst, trans.). London: Elephant.

Kropotkin, Peter (1987). *The state; Its historic role.* (Vernon Richards, trans.). London: Freedom Press.

Laclau, Ernesto, & Mouffe, Chantal (1985). *Hegemony and socialist strategy; Towards a radical democratic politics.* NY: Verso.

Lange, Oskar, & Taylor, Fred M. (1964). *On the economic theory of socialism.* New York: McGraw-Hill.

Lenin, V.I. (1970a). *Selected works* (vol. 1). Moscow: Progress Publishers.

Lenin, V.I. (1970b). *Selected works* (vol. 2). Moscow: Progress Publishers.

Lenin, V.I. (1979). *Selected works.* (vol. 3). Moscow: Progress Publishers.

Lincoln, Abraham. Quote. http://www.brainyquote.com/

Lindenfeld, Frank, & Rothschild-Whitt, Joyce (Eds.) (1982). *Workplace democracy and social change.* Boston: Porter Sargent Publishers.

Lovins, Amory B. (1977). *Soft energy paths: Toward a durable peace.* New York: Harper Colophon Books/Harper & Row.

Macdonald, Dwight (1957). *Politics past; Essays in political criticism.* New York: Viking Press. (Originally published as *Memoirs of a revolutionist.*)

Mackay, Louis, & Fernbach, David (Eds.) (1983). *Nuclear-free defence.* London: Heretic Books.

MacKinnon, Catharine A. (1989). *Toward a feminist theory of the state.* Cambridge MA: Harvard University Press.

McNally, David (1980). *Socialism from below .* Toronto: Workers' Acton Books.

McNally, David (2002). *Another world is possible: Globalization and anticapitalism.* Winnipeg: Arbeiter Ring.

McRobie, George (1981). *Small is possible.* New York: Harper & Row.

Makhno, Nestor (1996). *The struggle against the state and other essays.* Alexander Skirda (Ed.). San Francisco: AK Press.

Makhno, Nestor, Mett, Ida, Archinov, Piotr, Valevsky, & Linsky (1989). *Organizational platform of the libertarian communists.* Dublin: Workers Solidaraity Movement. (Copied in *Readings on building revolutionary anarchist organization.* [undated] New York: Love and Rage Revolutionary Anarchist Federation.)

Malatesta, Errico (1974). *Anarchy.* London: Freedom Press.

Malatesta, Errico (1984). *Errico Malatesta; His life and ideas* (3rd ed.). Vernon Richards (Ed.). London: Freedom Press.

Malatesta, Errico (1995). *The anarchist revolution; Polemical articles 1924-1931.* (V. Richards, ed.) London: Freedom Press..

Marx, Karl (1974a). *The First International and after; Political writings, vol. iii.* David Fernbach (Ed.). New York: Vintage Books/Random House.

Marx, Karl (1974b). *The revolutions of 1848; Political writings, vol. i.* David Fernbach (Ed.). New York: Vintage Books/Random House.

Marx, Karl, & Engels, Frederick (1971). *On the Paris Commune.* Moscow: Progress Publishers.

Maslennikov, V. (1983). *The co-operative movement in Asia and Africa* (Jane Sayer, trans.). Moscow: Progress Publishers

Mattack, Paul (1983). *Marxism: Last refuge of the bourgeoisie?* Armonk, NY: M.E. Sharpe.

Mbah, Sam, & Igariwey, I.E. (1997). *African anarchism: The history of a movement.* Tucson, AZ: See Sharp Press.

Mies, Maria (1986). *Patriarchy and accumulation on a world scale; Women in the international division of labor.* London, UK: Zed Books Ltd.

Miliband, Ralph (1969). *The state in capitalist society.* London: Weidenfeld & Nicolson.

Morris, David (1982). *The new city-states.* Washington, D.C.: Institute for Local Self-Reliance.

Morris, Mark (Ed.) (1976). *Instead of prisons; A handbook for abolitionists.* Syracuse, NY: Prison Research Education Action Project.

Morris, William (1986). *News from nowhere and selected designs.* (Asa Briggs, ed.). London: Penguin.

Morrison, Roy (1995). *Ecological democracy.* Boston: South End Press.

Morrow, Felix (1974). *Revolution and counterrevolution in Spain; including The civil war in Spain.* New York: Pathfinder Press.

Mouffe, Chantal (Ed.) (1992). *Dimensions of radical democracy; Pluralism, citizenship, community.* NY: Verso.

Mouffe, Chantal (1996). Radical democracy or liberal democracy? In D. Trend (Ed.). *Radical democracy.* NY: Routledge. (Pp. 19-26.)

Mumford, Lewis (1970). *The culture of cities.* New York: A Harvest/HBJ Book/Harcourt Brace Jovanovich.

Mumford, Lewis (1986). *The future of technics and civilization.* London: Freedom Press.

Nitze, Paul (1999, October 28). A threat mostly to ourselves. *The New York Times; Op-Ed*, p. A31.

Nove, Alec (1983). *The economics of feasible socialism.* London: George Allen and Unwin.

Orwell, George (1980). *Homage to Catalonia.* New York: Harcourt Brace Jovanovich--A Harvest/HBJ Book.

Ostergaard, Geoffrey (1997). *The tradition of workers' control.* London: Freedom Press.

Pannekoek, Anton (2003). *Workers' councils.* Oakland, CA: AK Press.

Paz, Abel (1976). *Durruti: The people armed* (trans. Nancy Macdonald). Montreal, Canada: Black Rose Books.

Peirats, Jose (1974). *Anarchists in the Spanish revolution.* Detroit: Black and Red.

Pepinsky, Harold E. & Quinney, Richard (Eds.) (1991). *Criminology as peacemaking.* Bloomington and Indianapolis: Indiana Universtiy Press.

Pipes, Richard (1990). *The Russian revolution.* New York: Knopf.

Price, Wayne (2000). Anarchism as extreme democracy. *The Utopian: A Journal of Anarchism and Libertarian Socialism.* Vol. 1. Pp. 32-42.

Radosh, Ronald, Habeck, Mary, & Sevostianov, Grigory (Eds.) (2001). *Spain betrayed: The Soviet Union in the Spanish civil war.* New Haven: Yale University Press.

Rabinowitch, Alexander (1968). *Prelude to revolution: The Petrograd Bolsheviks and the July 1917 uprising.* Bloomington: Indiana University Press.

Rabinowitch, Alexander (1976). *The Bolsheviks come to power: The revolution of 1917 in Petrograd.* NY: W.W. Norton.

Richards, Vernon (1972). Lessons of the Spanish revolution (1936--1939). London: Freedom Press.

Rivista Anarchica (1989). *Red years, black years; Anarchist resistance to fascism in Italy.* London: ASP.

Roberts, Adam (1976). *Nations in arms; The theory and practice of territorial defense.* New York: Praeger.

Roberts, Adam, Frank, Jerome, Naess, Arne, & Sharp, Gene (1964). *Civilian defence.* London, UK: Peace News.

Rothbard, M. N. (1978). *For a new liberty: The libertarian manifesto* (rev. ed.). New York: Collier Books/Macmillian.

Sale, Kirkpatrick (1980). *Human scale.* New York: Coward, McCann, & Geochegan.

Sale, Kirkpatrick (1985). *Dwellers in the land; The bioregional vision.* San Francisco: Sierra Club Books.

Schumacher, E.F. (1973). *Small is beautiful; Economics as if people mattered.* New York: Perennial Library/Harper & Row.

Schumacher, E.F. (1979). *Good work.* New York: Harper Torchbooks/Harper & Row.

Seymour, Joseph (2001). *Marxism vs. anarchism.* NY: Spartacist Publishing Company.

Shachtman, Max (1962). *The bureaucratic revolution: The rise of the Stalinist state.* NY: Donald Press.

Shalom, Stephen R. (2004). ParPolity: Political vision for a good society; draft. Life After Capialism essays. http://www.zmag.org/shalompo.htm.

Sherover-Marcuse, Erica (1986). *Emancipation and consciousness: Dogmatic and dialectical perspectives in the early Marx.* NY: Basil Blackwell.

Sirianni, Carmen (1982). *Workers' control and socialist democracy: The soviet experience.* London: Verso.

Skinner, B.F. (1962). *Walden two.* New York: Macmillan.

Skirda, Alexandre (2004). *Nestor Makhno, Anarchy's cossack; The struggle for free soviets   in the Ukraine 1917--1921.* (Paul Sharkey, trans.). London/Oakland CA: AK Press.

Smith, Dan (1982). *Non-nuclear military options for Britain.* London, UK: Housmans.

Spretnak, Charlene, & Capra, Fritjof (1986). *Green politics: The global promise.* Santa Fe, NM: Bear & Company.

Tabor, Ron (1988). *A look at Leninism.* New York: Aspect Foundation.

Tawney, R.H. (1948). *The acquisitive society.* New York: Harvest/Harcourt Brace Jovanovich.

Trend, David (Ed.) (1996). *Radical democracy; Identity, citizenship, and the state.* NY: Routledge.

Trotsky, Leon (1961). *Terrorism and communism: A reply to Karl Kautsky.* Ann Arbor, MI: University of Michigan Press.

Trotsky, Leon (1967). *The history of the Russian revolution* (trans. Max Eastman), in three volumes. London: Sphere Books.

Trotsky, Leon (1970a). *The permanent revolution* and *Results and prospects.* New York, Pathfinder Press.

Trotsky, Leon (1970b). *The revolution betrayed; What is the Soviet Union and where is it going?* New York: Merit/Pathfinder Press.

Trotsky, Leon (1971). *The struggle against fascism in Germany.* NY: Pathfinder Press.

Trotsky, Leon (1973). *The Spanish revolution (1931-39)* (eds. Naomi Allen and George Breitman). New York: Pathfinder Press.

Trotsky, Leon (1977). *The transitional program for socialist revolution.* New York: Pathfinder Press.

Tuchman, Barbara (1994). *The proud tower; A portrait of the world before the war 1890--1914.* NY: Ballantine Books.

Tucker, Benjamin R. (1888). *State socialism and anarchism; How far they agree and wherein they differ.* Alpine, MI: Charles W. Bergman.

van den Berg, Axel (1988). *The imminent utopia; From Marxism on the state to the state of Marxism.* Princeton NJ: Princeton University Press.

Voline (1974). *The unknown revolution; 1917-1921.* Montreal: Black Rose Books.

Watson, David (1997?). *Against the megamachine; Essays on empire and its enemies.* Brooklyn, NY: Autonomedia.

Watson, David (1996). *Beyond Bookchin; Essays for a future social ecology.* Brooklyn, NY: Autonomedia.

Wood, Ellen Meiksins (1995). *Democracy against capitalism; Renewing historical materialism.* Cambridge University Press.

Woodcock, George (1962). *Anarchism; A history of libertarian ideas and movements.* NY: World Publishing.

Index

W

What is Property? 165
withering-away of state 43, 51
women 4, 12, 15, 16, 18, 23, 27, 40,
    50, 101, 102, 112, 136, 167,
    174, 178
Women's Liberation 40, 102
Wood, Ellen Meiksins 15, 190
Woodcock, George 165, 190
working class 3, 4, 5, 18, 19, 21, 23,
    26, 31, 33, 35, 38, 39, 41, 44,
    45, 46, 48, 49, 51, 52, 53, 55,
    57, 102, 103, 104, 105, 112,
    113, 118, 127, 131, 133, 134,
    136, 141, 146, 147, 149, 151,
    152, 155, 156, 157, 158, 159,
    181
world government 75, 76, 105, 106

Y

Yugoslavia 62, 63, 64, 100, 126